York, South Carolina, Newspapers Marriage and Death Notices 1823-1865

Compiled by
BRENT H. HOLCOMB
C. A. L. S.

YORKVILLE ENQUIRER OFFICE.—Photographed by T. B. McClain.

THE REPRINT COMPANY, PUBLISHERS
Spartanburg, South Carolina
2010

Originally published: 1981
Reprinted: 1989
Print On Demand Edition: 2010
The Reprint Company, Publishers
Spartanburg, South Carolina

ISBN 978-0-87152-353-2
Library of Congress Catalog Card Number: 81-17743
Manufactured in the United States of America

The paper used in this publication meets the minimum
requirements of the American National Standard
for Information Sciences—Permanence of
Paper for Printed Library Materials
ANSI Z39.48-1992

Library of Congress Cataloging In Publication Data

Holcomb, Brent
York, South Carolina, newspapers, marriage, and death
notices, 1823-1865. Includes index.
1. York (S.C.)—Genealogy. 2. Registers of births, etc.—South
Carolina—York. 3. South Carolina—Genealogy. 4. Registers of
births, etc.—South Carolina. 5. North Carolina—Genealogy.
6. Registers of births, etc.—North Carolina. I. Title
F279.Y67H64   929'.375743   81-17743   AACR2

CONTENTS

INTRODUCTION

This volume contains abstracts of marriage and death notices from all extant newspapers of York (or Yorkville), South Carolina, which could be located. The vast majority of these are available at the South Caroliniana Library of the University of South Carolina in Columbia, to which we are indebted for their use. Where an issue is in a different location, this location is given after the date of the issue.

Unfortunately, the issues of the 1820s, 1830s, and 1840s have large gaps. However, because of the practice of the day of newspapers copying each other's notices, a perusal of newspapers of adjacent areas can provide some missing information. Because York District (now County) was a predominantly Presbyterian area, many notices of York residents are found in *Marriage and Death Notices from the Charleston Observer 1827–1845*, the *Charleston Observer* being a Presbyterian newspaper.

Of great interest to researchers are the many notices from the adjacent and nearby Union, Spartanburg, Lancaster, and Chester districts in South Carolina, and Cleveland, Gaston, and Mecklenburg counties in North Carolina. Probably a large number of North Carolinians came to Yorkville to marry to avoid the fee for a marriage bond or the delay in publishing banns, as was the statute in North Carolina.

Happily, the *Yorkville Enquirer* has extant a complete file of newspapers for the period of the Confederate War. Very few newspapers could continue publishing during this period for lack of available paper, and many of those which did publish have not survived. In addition to the obituaries of the soldiers, those of the older persons who died during the war are important. Often, money was scarce during and after the war, and tombstones were never erected for many of the people for whom we have obituaries here.

BRENT H. HOLCOMB

C.A.L.S.

15 May 1981

THE PIONEER

Issue of August 23, 1823 (Volume I, #2)

Married on Wednesday last by John Henry, Esq., Mr. William
Lee, late of Pee Dee, to Miss Margaret Brown, late of Tennessee.

Issue of August 30, 1823

Georgetown, S. C. Aug. 16 MELANCHOLY ACCIDENT. Last Sunday
a party returning from church, near Godfrey's ferry, were obliged
to take refuge from the impending storm in the house of Mr.
Daniel Davis--among them were Benjamin Avant and Miss Ann Philips.
Mr. Avant had reached the door, and Miss Philips was in the
act of entering the house, when a tree near them was struck by
lightning, the fluid passing through the house and instantly killed
them. Mrs. Davis received a severe shock but soon recovered. No
other person was affected by the lightning although the collection
was numerous.

Issue of September 13, 1823

Departed this life at his residence in this district, on Monday
morning last, about nine o'clock, David B. Rice, Esq. for several
years a respected citizen of this village. In the death of Mr.
Rice, society has to lament the loss of an amiable and very worthy
citizen, the correct course of whose conduct gained him the esteem
and confidence of all who had the pleasure of his acquaintance.
He leaves behind him a wife and three children to deplore the
loss of an affecionate husband and parent.

Issue of September 20, 1823

Died, Yesterday morning, at his residence in this District,
Dr. Robert L. Armstrong, aged about thirty years.
Married on Thursday evening last, by the Rev. Robert B. Walker,
Mr. George Steele, formerly of Chester, to Miss Mary Bratton, of
this place.

Issue of September 27, 1823

Married on Thursday last, by the Rev. R. B. Walker, Mr. Andrew
Hanna, to Miss Martha Byers, all of this District.
Died on the 14th inst. at his residence on the Beauty Spot,
Mr. William Thomson, in the 73d year of his age. As a man, Mr.
Thomson's merits were conspicuous; it was his maxim through life
that "An honest man is the greatest work of God." He possessed
the social and domestice feelings in an eminent degree; accordingly
in the different relations of husband, father, friend and master,
he was tender, affectionate, sincere and humane...His character
was formed and his principles fixed by the arduous toils of the
Revolution, in which he largely participated.... Under the celebrated Patrick Henry, he assisted in expelling Lord Dunmore from
Virginia....
Departed this life on Saturday the 20th instant, James Edwin
Williams, eldest son of the Rev. A. Williams, of Union district,
aged 8 years and 8 months. (verse).

Issue of October 4, 1823

Married on Thursday evening last, by Robert Davison, Esq., Mr.
_____ Anderson, of Union, to Miss Eleanor M'Cain, daughter of Mr.

1

James M'Cain of this district.

Died on Tuesday last, 30th ult., Thomas Campbell, Esq., assistant Sheriff of this District, in the 25th year of his age. His eulogy will be pronounced by all who knew him, and our feeble efforts will add nothing to the meed of praise which our citizens have justly awarded him.

Died on Wednesday, 1st inst., Mrs. Judith Carroll, consort of Mr. Hamilton Carroll, of this district.

Death of John W. Eppes. The Richmond Compiler of the September 17, says "The melancholy account reached us yesterday morning of the death of John W. Eppes, Esq. after a long and lingering indisposition. Mr. Eppes served in both branches of congress with distinguished reputation. He was respected by the people and beloved in all the walks of private life. For solid worth, he has not perhaps left his superior behind him."

Died at Philadelphia, Commodore John Shaw, the 8th oldest of the 30 Captains in the U. States' Navy, recently appointed to the command on the Charleston station.

Gen. Henry Lallemand, General of the Artillery of the late Imperial Guard of France, died the day before yesterday, at Bordenton, and was interred, this morning, in this city....Nat. Gaz. Sept. 16.

Issue of October 18, 1823

The celebrated CARNOT has died, after a painful illness, at Magdeburg, where he had taken refuge since 1815. He was one of those men who have done honor to France, and retained, amidst many seductions, his character for honesty and firmness. He was a member of the Executive Directory, and of the Academy of Sciences, and a Lieutenant-General in the French army. He accepted of no conspicuous public employment under the reign of Napoleon, till the French territory was invaded. He was born 13th May 1753.

Issue of November 1, 1823

Died at his residence in Union District, on the 15th ult., of a lingering disease, Henry Farnandis, in the 54th year of his age; He was a native of Charles county, State of Maryland.

Issue of November 8, 1823

Married on the 30th ult., by the Rev. E. Harris, Mr. Thomas C. M'Mahan, to Miss Eliza Wilson, both of this district.

Issue of November 15, 1823

Died in this village, on Monday morning last, of the Typhus Fever, Mr. John Hudson, in the 25th year of his age.

Issue of November 22, 1823

Died on Wednesday night the 12th instant at Columbia, S. C., Mr. Charles L. Cline, Printer, formerly of Philadelphia, but for a few years past a resident of the former place.

Issue of December 6, 1823

Married on Thursday the 27 Nov. by the Rev. Hugh M'Millan, Mr. William Wright, to Miss Mary Murphy, all of this District.

Issue of December 13, 1823

Married on Thursday the 4th inst., by J. M'Kee, Esq., Mr. Nathaniel O'Carrol, to Miss Jane Patton, all of this District.

Died on Tuesday the 25th ult., Mr. John Hart, Senior, near the O. N. Ford. His last sickness was lingering, and borne with patience. In sterling integrity he had few equals....

Issue of December 20, 1823

Married on Thursday the 11th inst., by the Rev. Eleazar Harris, Mr. Thomas Bailey, of this District, to Mrs. Sarah Gibson, of Mecklenburg County, N. C.

Married on the 25th ult., by John Henry, Esq., Mr. John Barnhill, to Miss Ann Brown, of this District.

Issue of January 3, 1824

Married on Thursday the 4th ult., by Elias Robertson, Esq., Mr. Thomas Thomason, to Miss Sarah, daughter of Maj. T. Roach, all of this district.

On Thursday 18th ult.,by James M'Kee, Esq., Mr. Alexander Faris, to Miss Jane Hagins, all of this district.

On Thursday 25th ult., by the same, Mr. Brown Duncan, of Kentucky, to Miss Rebecca Pittes, of this district.

On same day by the same, Mr. Henry Patterson, to Miss Cynthia Savil, all of this district.

On Tuesday 30th ult., Mr. William Adair, of Georgia, to Miss Susan Rooker, daughter of the Rev. Mr. Rooker.

Issue of January 17, 1824

Married on Saturday the 3d instant, by James M'Kee, Esq., Mr. Thomas Watson, to Miss Patsey Patterson, all of this District.

Also, on Thursday evening last, by the Reverend Josiah Harris, Mr. Stanhope Sadler, to Miss Mary Ann, daughter of Mr. B. Chambers, merchant, of this place.

Also, on Thursday the 8th instant by ____ Cherry, Esq., Mr. John A. Findley, to Miss Juliet Brown, all of Chester District.

Issue of January 24, 1824

Died near Marietta, (O), Rufus Putnam, aged about ninety, a Brigadier General by brevet, at the close of the Revolutionary War, and afterwards a Brigardier under Wayne, in the Western Army, formerly of Rutland, Mass. The Marquis La Fayette is now the solitary surviving General of the American Revolutionary Army.

Died at Rogersville, East Tennessee, on the 6th ult., Francis Dalzell, Esq., formerly Post-Master, and for many years a respectable merchant of that place. His relatives live in the City of Philadelphia, from which he emigrated many years ago.

Issue of January 31, 1824

Married on Thursday last, by Robert Smith, Esq., Mr. Wm. Garwin, to Miss Susannah Muller.

On Tuesday last by the Rev. Aron Williams, Mr. Wm. Jones,to Miss Elizabeth Davis, all of Union District.

On Tuesday last, Mr. Thomas Mason, to Miss Eliza Caston.

Issue of February 7, 1824

Married on Thursday the 22d ult., by Thomas M'Kee, Esq., Mr. Hugh Venable, to Miss Elizabeth Turner, all of this district.

Issue of February 14, 1824

Married on Thursday evening last, by J. Henry, Esq., Mr. Andrew Baxter, to Violet Baron, all of this district.

Died on Tuesday, the 10th inst., at the residence of Dr. Edmund Jennings, his mother, Mrs. Elizabeth Jennings, of a very advanced age. The deceased was for a series of years, a professing member of the Methodist Church, and showed by her exemplary conduct the might efficacy of the atoning blood of the "Lamb of God...."

Issue of February 21, 1824

Married on the 12th inst., by the Rev. R. B. Walker, Capt. William L. Wallace, to Miss Jane G. Boyd, both of Chester District.

Issue of February 28, 1824

Married on Thursday the 18th inst., by the Rev. William G. Davis, Dr. Thomas Brown, of Chester, to Miss Prudence Feemster, of York District.

On the same day, by John Henry Esq., Mr. C. Pierce, to Miss Mary Gabbie.

On the same day, by the same, Mr. Walten Moore, to Miss _____ Hayes.

On the same day, by the same, Mr. _____ Jones, to Miss _____ Hayes.

Issue of March 20, 1824

Married by the Rev. Charles Strong, on the 4th instant, Capt. Christopher Strong, of Chester, to Miss Martha H. Harris, daughter of Capt. John Harris, of this district.

By the Rev. Josiah Harris, on Thursday the 11th inst., Mr. George Albert Smart, of Mecklenburg, N. C. to Miss Mary Wethers, daughter of Maj. Benjamin Wethers, of Lancaster, in this state.

Issue of April 3, 1824

Married on Tuesday last, by John Henry, Esq., Mr. Jas. McDowell, of Spartanburgh, to Miss Mary Ann Ferguson, daughter of Col. Wm Ferguson, of this District.

Issue of April 10, 1824

Died on Wednesday last, Samuel, the infant son of Samuel Melton, of the measles, aged two years and six months.

Issue of April 17, 1824

Died of the Measles, at his residence in this District, on the 12th instant, Col. James Clendinen, in the 53d year of his age. He left an affectionate wife and two little infants, with many relatives and sincere friends to deplore his loss....(eulogy)

THE PIONEER

Issue of April 24, 1824

Married on the evening of the 18th of this month, by the
Rev. Robert M. Davis, Mr. Robert S. Coln, to Miss Jane L. Gaston,
both of Chester District.

Issue of May 15, 1824

Died, in Philadelphia, on the 28th ult., in the 36th year of
his age, Captain Joseph Stout Macpherson, of the U. S. Navy, son
of the late Gen. Wm. Macpherson.

Issue of June 26, 1824

Died on Sunday evening the 20th inst., Mrs. Anne Davis, consort of Mr. George Davis, of this vicinity.
On Wednesday, the 23d inst., William, son of Mr. John Chambers,
of this vicinity, aged about 8 years.

Issue of July 3, 1824

Died on Sunday evening, the 20th inst., after an illness of
nine days, in the sixty-second year of her age, Mrs. Anne Davis,
consort of Mr. George Davis, of this vicinity. (long eulogy)
In York District, on Tuesday the 22d ult., Mr. John Cooper,
in the eighty-fifth year of his age. Also, on Saturday, the 26th,
his wife, Mrs. Elizabeth Cooper, in the eighty-seventh year of
her age....having spent upwards of sixty years together.... The
education and welfare of their children, formed the principal
object of their lives.... (eulogy)

Issue of July 10, 1824

Married on Sunday the 27th inst., by Henry Meacham, Esq., Mr.
Daniel Green M'Clamore, of Lancaster District, to the amiable
Miss Margaret Hull of York District.
On Tuesday the 8th inst., by the Rev'd John Rooker, Mr.
Nathl. Harris to Miss Sarah Pettus, both of York District.

Issue of July 31, 1824

Married on Thursday evening, July 22d, 1824, by Joseph McKenzie,
Esq., Mr. Aaron Wood, to Miss Matilda Mayhue.

THE PIONEER AND SOUTH-CAROLINA WHIG

N. B. The following issues are at the Library of Congress,
Washington, D. C.

Issue of July 4, 1829

The late Major Charles Miles...on the 13th of March last bid
a last adieu to all terrestrial things...(a petition to the legislature telling of Charles Miles's service in the Revolution was
published by his friends after his death. He had asked for com-
pensation and was rejected).
Married on the 2nd inst., by Samuel Berry, Esq., Mr. Joseph
Harper, to Miss Margaret Currence, daughter of Mr. Hugh Currence,
all of this district.

Issue of August 1, 1829

Mr. Coleman, for many years the editor of the N. Y. Evening Post, died a few days since, in New York, in the 64th year of his age.

Died in Unionville, on Friday evening the 24th ultimo, Miss Sarah Jane, daughter of John and Martha Gage, in the 13th year of her age....(eulogy).

Issue of August 8, 1829

Died on the 17th ult., in Washington, Autauga County, Alabama, the Rev. G. G. M'Whorter, in the 67th year of his age, formerly of this state. He was one of the patriots of the Revolution....

Issue of September 5, 1829

Married on Thursday evening last, by the Rev. W. C. Hill, Mr. Matthew Hogg, to Miss Mary, daughter of Mr. John Chambers, all of this district.

Died on Tuesday last, Mr. James McClain, of this district. He was a soldier of the late war, in which he lost one of his arms.

In Charlotte, N. C., on Thursday the 27th ultimo, Joseph Wilson, Esq., an eminent citizen and distinguished lawyer.

Issue of October 24, 1829

Married on Thursday the 8th inst., by the Rev. Samuel Williamson, Mr. S. H. Elliott of this district, to Mrs. Mary Smart, of Mecklenburg, N. C.

On the 1st inst., by the Rev. Thomas Wright, Reuben Pickett, Esq. attorney at law, to Miss Mary J. Dismukes, daughter of Col. William Dismukes.

On Thursday the 15th inst., by M. T. Hall, Esq., Mr. Milton Garison, to Miss Ann Faris, all of York District.

On Thursday the 8th inst., by M. T. Hall, Esq., Mr. Mark Garison, to Miss Lucretia Garison, all of this District.

Died in this District, on the 14th inst., Thomas Carroll, in the 93d year of his age. The deceased was a distinguished soldier of the Revolution.

On Tuesday morning last, at the house of Dr. McKenzie, in Cabarrus County, N. C., Miss Eliza Lucinda McCall, of this village. (eulogy).

Issue of December 11, 1830

Married on Tuesday evening last, by the Rev. R. Y. Russell, Mr. Wm. Giles to Miss Catharine C. McDaniel, all of York District.

On the same evening, Mr. G. B. Tracy, to Miss Nancy Robertson, both of Union.

On the same evening, Mr. W. Harris, to Miss Sarah Harris, both of Union.

On the same evening, Capt. J. Palmore, aged 81, to Mrs. Rhody Porter, aged 76, both of Union.

Issue of January 9, 1830

Another foul deed--on the night of the 27th November, Mr. William Foster, Jr., of this county...engaged in a social converse with his wife and only child, was shot through the heart... of which he instantly expired....   Claiborne Alabama Herald

Married on Tuesday the 15th ult., by T. Hall, Esq., Mr. Charles Anderson, to Miss Judah Smith.

On Thursday the 17th ult., by the Rev. J. S. Adams, Mr. Mylas Smith, to Miss Rebecca Patrick, all of this district.

On the same day by the Rev. L. S. Watson, Dr. A. L. Barry, of Lancaster district, to Miss Margaret M'Dowall, of Mecklenburg Co., N. C.

On the same day by J. M'Corkle, Esq., Mr. Hugh M'Cain of Georgia, to Miss Elizabeth Douglass, of this district.

On Thursday the 31st ult., by the Rev. James S. Adams, Mr. John N. Currence to Miss Martha P. Barnett, all of this District.

On Thursday the 7th inst., by the Rev. Samuel Watson, Mr. Damuel M. Watson, to Miss Lucretia Hogge, all of this district.

Died at his residence in York district, on the 3d inst., Mr. Robert Pilcher, about 75 years of age... (eulogy).

On the 2d inst., in this district, Dr. Wm. Miskelly, in the 70th year of his age.

Issue of October 29, 1825 (Vol. I, #4)

Married on Thursday last, by the Rev. Cyrus Johnston, Xerxes H. Cushman, Esq., one of the editors of this paper, to Miss Jane Dinkens, of Mecklenburg, N. C.

In Rutherford, N. C. on Tuesday evening last, by the Rev. Mr. Moore, Dr. Edmund Jennings, of this village, to Miss Mary Burchett.

In Mecklenburg, N. C. on Thursday evening, 18th inst., by the Rev. Mr. Roper, Mr. Washington Morrison, to Miss Mary Dinkens.

Died on Saturday, 22d inst., Martha Caroline, infant daughter of Mr. Ephraim A. Crenshaw, of this village.

Issue of November 5, 1825

Married in Salisbury, N. C. on Tuesday the 1st inst., by the Rev. Mr. Freeman, Mr. William C. Beatty, of Yorkville, to Miss Nancy Yarbrough, of the former place.

Issue of November 26, 1825

Married in this District, on the 24th inst., by the Rev. Cyrus Johnston, William C. Penick, M. D. of Va. to Miss Elizabeth Narcissa Byers.

Issue of January 14, 1826

Died on the 27th ult., at the seat of Dr. John Scott, about 3 miles from Salisbury, Mrs. Eliza Scott, wife of the Doctor, in the 27th year of her age. Mrs. Scott was an amiable and highly esteemed woman--as much as as deservedly so, as any lady in the county. She has left a kind and affectionate husband, two small children and an extensive circle of relatives and friends, to deplore her decease.

Issue of January 21, 1826

From the N. Y. Evening Post, Jan. 5.
MELANCHOLY ACCIDENT. Mr. John S. Fox, of Mecklenburg county, North Carolina, aged about 25 years, a member of the Medical Institution of this city, walked off the bridge at the Ferry, fott of Barclay street this morning and was drowned. Mr. Fox had been attending the lectures during the winter, but on account of ill health was obliged to leave the city, and arose before six o'clock this morning and in company with a fellow student was proceeding to the steam boat to cross the river and take the state for the southward, intending to return home....

Issue of February 11, 1826

Married on the 19th ult., by the Rev. J. S. Adams, Mr. J. B. Patterson, of Lincoln, N. C. to Miss F. C. McCully of this District.

On Thursday the 2d inst., by the Rev. Josiah Harris, Mr. I. N. Sadler to Miss Mary W. Litle, all of this district.

On Thursday last, by the Rev. Cyrus Johnston, Mr. J. H. Suggs, to Miss Tabitha Youngblood, all of this District.

Issue of March 11, 1826

Just as our paper was going to press, we received the painful

intelligence of the death of the Hon. John Gaillard, Senator in
Congress from this state. He died at Washington on the 26th ult.
full of years and honor... from the Columbia Telescope.

A coroner's inquest was held upon the body of John M. Galligher, which was found dead in the road about five miles east of
this place on Monday evening last. He had been in town on the
preceding day, and was on his return home when the accident
happened...The inquest returned a verdict, that the said John M.
Galligher came to his death by a fall from his horse when intoxi-
cated...(long editorial).

Issue of March 18, 1826

Married on Thursday last in this vicinity by Robert Davidson,
Esq., Mr. John Brady of this place, to Miss Isabella Garvin, of
this District.

Issue of April 15, 1826

Married on Thursday last, by the Rev. John Rooker, Mr. N. T.
Green of Warrenton, N. C. to Miss Sarah C. C. Dinkins, of Mecklenburg, N. Carolina.

Died in Camden on the 6th inst., of the prevailing influenza
William Ennis, Printer, a native of New-bern, North-Carolina,
aged 32 years.

Issue of April 29, 1826

Departed this life on Saturday the 15th inst., Milton M. N.
McMahan, son of Mr. Daniel McMahan, of Pinckneyville, aged 14
years.

At a meeting of the Trustees of Unity Accadamy, occasioned
by the death of Milton N. M. McMahan, one of the Students, who
departed this life 15th inst., it was resolved that the students
wear crape on the left arm, for one month at School....that a
funeral sermon, adapted to the occasion, be, immediately after
the eulogy, delivered by the Rev. A. Williams.

John S. Moore, Sec.

Issue of July 22, 1826

Married on Tuesday the 18th inst., by the Rev. Robert B.
Walker, Isaac D. Witherspoon, Esq. of this place, to Miss Ann
T. K. Reid, of this District.

In this place, on Sunday last, between the hours of 12 and
1 o'clock, Mary Eliza, infant daughter of Mr. John H. DeCarteret.

Issue of August 19, 1826

Died in Iredell County, N. C., on the 25th of July, the Rev.
James Hall, D. D., aged 82.

Issue of August 26, 1826

From the Missouri Republican, July 20. Died in this city,
on Friday evening last, Horatio Cozens, Esq., an eminent attorney
and Counsellor at law, of this city. His death was produced in
consequence of wounds from a dirk, inflicted by French Strother,
a young man of this City, who was immediately arrested.

Issue of August 26, 1826 (contd.)

From the Western Carolinian. Died in Iredell county, N. C.
on the 25th of July, the Rev. James Hall, D. D., aged 82; for many
years the able, zealous and successful Pastor of the United
Presbyterian Churches of Concord, Fourth Creek and Bethany in
that county. (eulogy).

Issue of September 2, 1826

Died in this village on Thursday evening last, Mr. John J.
Chambers, aged 23 years--son of Benjamin Chambers, Esq.

Issue of September 9, 1826

Married on Tuesday evening the 29th ult., by the Rev. Mr.
Clifton, Mr. William Myers, to Miss Eliza, daughter of Major
John M'Lemore, of Richland District.

Issue of September 23, 1826

Died on Monday 18th inst., Mrs. Nancy Black, wife of Mr.
Thomas Black, of Union District. (eulogy).

Issue of September 30, 1826

Died in this place, on Thursday the 26th instant, Robert
Clendinen, Jun. infant son of the Hon. Robert Clendinen, aged
nine months and twenty three days, after a severe illness of
thirty three days. He was a child of extraordinary promise.
On the night of the 25 inst., after a short illness, Mrs.
Mary Carothers, consort of Mr. John Carothers, of Union District,
S. C. (eulogy).

Issue of October 7, 1826

Married in Mecklenburg County, N. C., on Thursday evening
last, by the Rev. Humphrey Hunter, Mr. James McWhorter, of this
place, to Miss Catharine Louisa McKnight. `
Near Fayetteville, N. C. on the 14th ult., Mr. Malcom McLean,
aged 21, to Miss Ann Mailor Snow, aged 11 !!!!

Issue of February 18, 1837

Departed this life on Wednesday evening last, at the residence of his son (A. McWhorter, Esq.) near the Village, Mr. Hugh Mc-Whorter, aged 81 years. The deceased was a native of Ireland, but for many years a citizen of this District. Venerated for his years, his firmness, patriotism and great goodness of heart, he has been followed to the grave by several friends; who will, at all times commemorate the memory of a beloved old man, of humble pretensions--who has suffered much in life, and much in death--but who at the hour of dissolution, perfectly resigned to the GREAT I AM, gave up the ghost without a murmur. Tears of affectionate connexions drop upon his grave, and bid him rest in peace.

On Friday the 10th inst., at his residence in this District, after a long and painful illness, Mr. John Barnwell, aged about 65 years.

Issue of June 1, 1840 (Vol. I, #1) [issue at UNC, Chapel Hill]

Married on the evening of the 21st ult., by the Rev. Daniel
Button, Mr. John McKoy, to Mrs. Sarah Quinn, all of this village.
On the evening of the 21st ult., by the Rev. P. E. Bishop, Mr.
William J. Bowen, to Miss Jane, daughter of Nathan Kimbril, all of
Ebenezer.
On Thursday last, by the Rev. James S. Adams, Mr. Nelson G.
Thomasson, to Miss Emily, daughter of William Youngblood, all of
this district.
Died in this District on yesterday the 31st ult., Mr. Joseph
Burns, aged about 38 years.

Issue of June 8, 1840

Married on the 7th ult., by the Rev. G. W. Davis, Mr. John
Guyton, of Union, to Miss Adeline, daughter of John Whisonant, of
this District.
On the 28th ult., by the same, Mr. Andrew K. Henry, of York,
to Miss Elizabeth, daughter of Reese Parker, of Union District.
In Chesterville, on Tuesday evening, the 19th ult., by the
Rev. John Douglas, Andrew B. Conley, Esq. to Miss Ellen, daughter
of John Rosborough, Esq.
Died in this place, on Monday last, Mr. James Tomlinson, in
the 37th year of his age.

Issue of June 13, 1840

Died in the Indian Land on the 7th instant, after a short
illness, Mr. Thomas H. Parish, in the 27th year of his age. He
has left a disconsolate wife and three small children to moan his
irreparable loss.

Issue of June 20, 1840

Married on the 17th inst., by the Rev. James Buoys, the Rev.
Laughlin McDonald of Chester District, to Miss Margaret, daughter
of Mr. Robert Brice of Fairfield District.
Died in this district on Saturday the 13th inst., William
Harvey, infant son of James Bigham.

Issue of June 27, 1840

Died in this District on Thursday the 18th inst. after an
illness of but a few days, Mrs. Martha J. Wright, consort of Mr.
James Lessley Wright, in the 29th year of her age, leaving a
husband and two small children to moan her loss.

Issue of July 11, 1840

Married on Tuesday the 30th ult. by John McKnight, Esq. Mr.
William Bratton, to Miss Isabella J. E., daughter of Capt. Jona-
than R. Hodd, all of this District.
Died in York District, South Carolina, on the 24th day of
June 1840, the Rev. John Rooker, in the 86th year of his age.
He was a true Soldier during the Revolutionary struggle for
Liberty, as a Volunteer against the Indian and Scotch Tories. He
was also, an old an firm Soldier in the cause of his Lord and
Master, having been engaged in ministerial duties as Pastor 48
years, at Flint Hill Baptist Church, S. C., during which period

he done honor to himself....   Charlotte Journal
     Died, at the residence of Capt. Thos. Kilpatrick, on Satur-
day the sixth of June, Mr. Robert Kilpatrick, a revolutionary
soldier, aged one hundred and five years. He was a native of
Ireland and emigrated to this country with his parents when
quite young. For the last eighty years he has been a citizen of
the districts of Chester and Fairfield. He served as a soldier
from the commencement till the close of the revolutionary war.
Sumter was his General, and Nixon and Adams his Captains. For
some time past he has been rewarded for his services by an annual
pension.... Carolina Planter.

Issue of July 18, 1840

     Died in this District on the 19th ult., Mr. Daniel Gilmore,
aged about 80 years. He was a revolutionary veteran, and served
during the war. Mr. Gilmore retained very good health till with-
in a few hours of his death.

Issue of August 15, 1840

     Married on Thursday evening last, in this place, by the Rev.
Robert Y. Russell, Mr. Daniel F. Hall, Merchant, of Blairsville,
to Miss Mary A. eldest daughter of James Brian Jr., Esquire.
     Married on the same evening, near this place by the Rev. Jehu
G. Postell, Mr. William A. Wallace, of this Village, to Miss
Jane A. Russell.

Issue of August 22, 1840

     Married on Tuesday the 18th inst., by the Rev. L. McDonald,
Robert C. Grier, of Mecklenburg County, N. C., to Miss Barbary
B., daughter of William Moffat Esq. of Chester District.
     Died in this district on Tuesday the 18th inst., Mr. Isaac
Kuykendal, aged about 42 years.

Issue of August 8, 1840

     Married on the 28th ultimo, by the Rev. W. B. Davis, Mr.
James Wood (of the Theological Seminary at Columbia) to Miss
Eliza Ann, daughter of the Rev. Aaron Williams of this District.

Issue of August 29, 1840

     Died in the Indian Land, on Sunday the 23rd inst., Mrs. Mary
Clawson, consort of Dr. J. H. Clawson, aged 50 years.
     In this place on Monday last, John Anderson, youngest son of
Thomas H. and Jaley Smith, aged 1 year and 8 months.

Issue of September 12, 1840

     Died in this place on Wednesday evening the 8th inst., after
a long and painful illness, Mrs. Elizabeth Erwin, consort of Capt.
William Erwin, in the 61st year of her age.
     Drowned--On Thursday the 27th August, in Broad River, at
Hamilton's Ford, Enoch McClain, of this neighborhood, in the 47th
year of his age. He had attempted to cross the river by swimming
and had nearly reached the opposite short, when it is supposed he
was taken with a cramp. His remains were found immediately, and
was buried at Hamilton's Grave Yard, in Union District....

Issue of September 26, 1840

Married on Wednesday last, by the Rev. William M. Wightman, Rev. James W. Welborn to Miss Minerva, eldest daughter of Gordan Moore, dec.

On Tuesday evening last, by _____ Abernathy, Esq., Mr. Silas H. Philips, of Union S. C. to Miss Joann Stroup, of Lincoln N. C.

On Monday last at Wilkinsville, by Aaron Wilkins, Esq., Mr. Thompson Harris of Union, S. C. to Miss Martha Mangum, late of Georgia.

Died at his residence, in Chesterville, on the 8th inst., Col. G. B. Colvin, very unexpectedly, after a short illness. He was near entering upon his 45th year, and was a man of robust, and healthy appearance.... The deceased was born in the District in which he died...He was for a length of time a Representative in the State Legislature, and afterwards a State Senator and served also in several militia offices, and was twice called to the command of the 26th Regiment, in this District as their Colonel. leaving a wife and five orphan children....

In this district at the residence of her son (James Hemphill) on the 15th inst., after a long and lingering illness, Mrs. Mary Hemphill, wife of Alexander Hemphill, dec., in the 100th year of her age.

Issue of October 1, 1840

Died in this Village on Thursday the 24th ult., Mrs. Isabella Porter, consort of Abner A. Porter, in the 24th year of her age. Also on Monday 28th ult., John Anderson, infant son of Abner A. Porter, aged about three months.

In this district, a few days since, after a short illness, Mr. Robert M'Carter, in the 58th year of his age.

In this city, on Sunday night last, of an abscess of the liver, in the 63rd year of his age, Beverly Daniel, Adjutant General of this State, and late Marshall of the United States for the District of North Carolina--which office he had held more than thirty years.--Microcosm.

Issue of October 10, 1840

Died on the 25th of September, ult. at his residence near Smithford in this District, Daniel Smith, Esq., at the age of sixty one years. It is worth of notice that he was sixty one, not merely to a day, but to an hour....left an afflicted family ...member of the Methodist Church.

Issue of October 24, 1840

Died in this District on the 30th ultimo, after an illness of a few days, Mr. Thomas Carroll, in the 26th year of his age.

In this District on the 12th inst., Miss Mary Sandifer, daughter Green Sandifer, in the 21st year of her age.

In this District, on the 12th inst., Mr. William Latimore, in the 24th year of his age--for the last four years, previous to his death a resident of Mississippi.

In Arkansas in the month of August last, Mr. Samuel W. M'Whorter, formerly of this place, in the 25th year of his age.

Issue of November 21, 1840

Fatal Affray. A sudden rencontre occurred in the streets
of thsi Village, Friday evening last, between Mr. Thomas B. Bird
and Col. Louis T. Whigfall, in the course of which, pistols were
mutually discharged. One of the shots inflicted a mortal wound
upon the former of these young gentlemen, of which he died Sunday
morning.... Edgefield Advertiser, Nov. 5.

Issue of December 12, 1840

Another Revolutionary Soldier Gone. Died at his residnece
in the Indian Land, near the Nation Ford, on the 29th November,
Mr. Thaddeus Shurley, aged 83 years, 3 months and 4 days.
Died at Lyme (Conn.) on the 29th ult., Captain Ezra Lee,
aged 72, a revolutionary officer. (long account). Phil. Saturday
Courier.

Issue of January 2, 1841

Married in this place on Thursday evening the 24th ult., by
Theodore Fulton Esq. Mr. Washington S. Bird, to Miss Amanda, eldest daughter of Daniel James, Esq.
Suicide. On Sunday evening, the 20th instant, a man whose
name from papers found in his possession, is supposed to be
Robert B. Hamilton, put an end to his earthly existence, at the
house of James M. Smith, in this Village, by hanging himself...
From papers found in his possession, it is supposed he had here-
tofore resided in Abbeville, South Carolina, and that he had
recently been at Spartanburg C. H.... Asheville, N. C. Messenger,
Dec. 25, 1840.

Issue of January 9, 1841

Died in this District on the 17 ultimo, Mary Jane, eldest
daughter of Hugh & Elizabeth A. Venable, in the 17th year of her
age.

Issue of January 23, 1841

Married on Wednesday evening last, by Rev. R. Y. Russel, Mr.
Edward M. Chambers, to Miss Hester J. Postell, all of this district.

Issue of January 29, 1841

Married in this place on Thursday evening last, by James
Jefferys Esq. Mr. Burret T. Wheeler, to Mrs Frances M. Henley,
all of this district.

Issue of February 12, 1841

Married on Tuesday evening last, by the Rev. Mr. Bishop, Mr.
Sylvanus W. Williamson, to Miss Sarah P., youngest daughter of
Richard Strait, all of this District.

15

Issue of March 19, 1841

Married on the 11th inst., by Peyton B. Darwin, Esq.,Mr.
Charles E. Wilkinson, to Miss Sarah Mariah Smith.

Issue of March 26, 1841

Married on Sunday evening the 21st inst., by A. McCullough,
Esq., Mr. John R. Nicholson, to Miss Elizabeth R., daughter of
Mr. A. R. Nicholson, all of Chesterville.
Died in Lancaster District on the 14th inst., Miss Ellen
Hunter, in the 17th year of her age!

Issue of April 2, 1841

Married on Sunday evening the 28th ult.,by Rev.G. W. Davis,
Maj. John Dennis, to Miss Margaret E. McElmoyle, all of this
district.

Issue of April 9, 1841

From the Columbia Southern Chronicle, April 7, 1841. Death
of President Gen. Harrison.

Issue of April 16, 1841

Married on Tuesday last in this place, by the Rev. Robert Y.
Russel, Dr. Hazel H. Smith, of Chester District, to Miss Martha
Emily, daughter of Capt. Wm. M. Erwin.
Died in this District on Thursday the 8th inst., Miss Sillis
Steedman, in her 17th year, daughter of William & Isabiah Steed-
man.
On last Sunday night, Mrs. Elizabeth Jones, consort of Dudley
Jones, in her 37th year.

Issue of April 23, 1841

Married on Thursday 22d, by the Rev. Samuel Townsend, Mr.
James F. Carson, of this place, to Miss Martha, daughter of Mr.
James Miskelly, of this vicinity.

Issue of May 15, 1841

Married in this place on Thursday 13th instant, by Wm. I.
Clawson, Esq., Mr. David Peterson (Printer), of Lincolnton, to
Miss Jane Rogers, of this place.

Issue of May 21, 1841

Married on Sunday the 16th inst., by A. McCullough, Esq., Mr.
Daniel Carroll to Miss Margaret Carroll, all of Chesterville.
Died in this District, on the 19th inst.,Mrs. Elizabeth
Neely, consort of Samuel Neely, dec'd., in her 76th year.

Issue of January 22, 1851

Married in this place on Monday morning last, by Rev. Mr. Little, Mr. Wm. M'Cloud, to Mrs. Stacey Plexico, all of this Village.

On Thursday the 16th inst., by Jas. Jefferys, Esq., Mr. James H. Wallis, to Miss Mary Clark, all of this District.

Died in this District on the 16th inst., Mrs. Lucy Traylor, aged about 35 years.

Issue of February 1, 1851

Died at his residence near Chesterville, on the ___, Mr. Robert Robinson, aged 55 years and 4 months.

Issue of February 15, 1851

Married on Tuesday the 11th inst., by James Jefferys Esquire, Mr. John Peters to Miss Sarah Jane Holmes, all of this District.

Issue of February 24, 1851

Married on Tuesday the 11th inst., by the Rev. S. L. Watson, Mr. Daniel Currence to Miss Mary Patrick, all of this District.

Died in this District on Sunday the 16th inst., Mrs. Margaret Hemphill, in the 65th year of her age.

In this District on Friday last (suddenly), Mr. Alfred McCall, aged about fifty years.

Issue of March 8, 1851

Married in this village, on the 4th inst., by Rev. R. Y. Russell, Mr. Samuel E. Moore, to Miss Anna C. Sadler, all of this village.

Issue of March 29, 1851

Married on Thursday the 27th inst., by James Jefferys Esquire, Mr. Wm. H. McDaniel to Miss Mary Turner, all of this District.

Issue of April 19, 1851

Married on the 17th instant, by P. B. Darwin, Esq., Mr. John Nickols, to Miss Rebecca Morgan, all of this District.

Issue of April 26, 1851

Death of Mr. Wm. Moffatt. We learned last week, after our paper went to press, of the death of our esteemed fellow citizen, Mr. William Moffatt...leaves to his family a large and well ordered estate...Chester Standard.

Issue of May 10, 1851

Died at the residence of Col. C. S. Sims, in Union District, on Saturday, 3d of May, Mrs. Catharine Quay, in the hundredth year of her age. She was a native of Cookstown, Ireland. In her decease she has left a large circle of relations and friends to mourn her loss. Chester Standard.

Issue of May 17, 1851

Died at his residence in this District, on Tuesday the 13th inst., James Simril, Sen., in the 75th year of his age. A worthy and respectable citizen.

Near this place, on the 15th inst., Mrs. Elizabeth Çraig, consort of John D. Craig, in the 40th year of her age.

Issue of May 24, 1851

Married in this place on Thursday the 22d instant by James Jefferys, Esq. Mr. R. L. Adams to Miss Mary A. Wholbrooks, all of this District.

Died near Yorkville on the 15th inst., William Harrison, youngest son of E. P. & Elizabeth Williams, aged about 2 years.

In this District on Sunday 18th inst., Mr. Alexander Barnett, in the 77th year of his age.

Issue of May 31, 1851

Died at his residence in Camden, Madison County, Mississippi, on Tuesday the 15th April, of Pneumonia, Dr. John LaFayette McCool, in the 37th year of his age, leaving a mourning widow and three small children to bewail their irrepairable loss.

On the day following, Elizabeth M'Cool, the mother of the deceased, aged 62 years, leaving a disconsolate husband behind her. Canton (Miss.) Madisonian.

Issue of June 7, 1851

Died in this place on Tuesday the 4th inst., Mr. John McKoy (Tanner), in the 51st year of his age.

In this place on the 2d inst., Mrs. Sarah Adickes, in the 65th year of her age.

At Cedar Hill, near Frankfort, Kentucky, on the 12th of May, Mrs. Anna Innis, relict of the Hon. Henry Innis, and mother of Mrs. J. J. Crittenden. This lady was one of the pioneers of Kentucky... Her early days were spent in the wilderness, and in the society of such men as Clarke, St. Clark, Wayne, Shelby, Scott (of the battle of Monmouth).... She saw Washington as he led his broken army through the Jerseys, and as he returned in triumph from Yorktown.

Issue of June 28, 1851

Died near Bethel, on Friday the 20th inst., William B. Jackson, Esq., in the 36th year of his age.

Issue of July 5, 1851

Died in this place on Saturday morning, the 28th ult., Mr. Robert Morrow in the 74th year of his age.

In this district on the 2d inst., Robert Allison, second son of T. J. & E. P. Clinton, in the 10th year of his age.

Issue of September 20, 1851

Died on the 8th instant, at Springfield, York District, S. C., John Springs, infant son of A. B. & Julia B. Springs, aged 10 months.

Issue of October 4, 1851

Departed this life on Thursday evening the 18th ult., Mrs. Sarah B., consort of Wm. J. Wilson, Esq., of Gaston Co., N. C., in the 79th year of her age. She was an affectionate parent, a kind neighbor and a most devoted friend. She has left behind an aged partner, a large family of children and grand-children, and a large circle of neighbors and friends...a member of the Presbyterian Church....

Issue of October 25, 1851

Married at Charlotte, N. C., on Tuesday morning, 21st inst., by Rev. Cyrus Johnson, Mr. Jerome B. Kerr, of Yorkville, to Miss Jane E. Johnson, of the former place.

Issue of November 15, 1851

Died at Middleburg, Tennessee, of Typhoid Fever, after an illness of only 16 days, Dr. Martin C. Brian (eldest son of James Brian Esq. of York District), in the 30th year of his age.

Issue of November 22, 1851

Sudden Death. On Monday evening last, shortly after dark, the body of Henry McCord, an Irish shoemaker, was found lying dead at the steps of Mr. Thompson's shoe-shop in this place. He was an intemperate man, and had recently been drinking very freely.... Chester Standard, 19 inst.

Account of Samuel Fleming being killed by Col. W. W. Avery at Morganton, N. C.

Issue of December 6, 1851

Married on Tuesday the 4th inst., by James Jefferys, Esq., Mr. Joseph A. Purseley to Miss Elizabeth McDaniel, all of this district.

Died in Marshall county, Mississippi, on the 24th of November last, Dr. Wm. McGowan, formerly of Pinckneyville, S. C., aged about 51 years.

Issue of December 13, 1851

Married on Thursday the 11th instant by Rev. S. L. Watson, Mr. David Hemphill of Georgia, to Miss Isabella Carrol of this Dis-trict.

Issue of January 10, 1852

Married in Winnsboro' on the 6th inst., by the Rev. S. L. Watson, Rev. Andrew M. Watson, of York District, to Miss Martha A. Campbell of the former place.

Died in Augusta, Ga., on the 20th of November, Mrs. Delila Farrar, aged about 48 years; consort of Mr. George Farrar, former-

ly of York District, S. C.
In Yorkville, on Monday morning, 5th inst., Capt. Joshua D. Goore, aged 63 years and 7 months.

Issue of March 27, 1852

Married on Thursday morning, the 25th inst., by Rev. J. M. H. Adams, Mr. Thomas B. Frazier, of Sumter District, S. C., to Miss Sarah Margaret McIver, of this place.
On Sunday evening the 21st int., by Joseph M'Cosh, Esq., Mr. Willis White, to Miss Celia Bridges, all of this District.

Issue of April 10, 1852

Father Brocard the head of the order of Jesuits in this country died at Georgetown Convent on Friday.

Issue of May 8, 1852

Married on Tuesday the 29th ult., by Rev. W. B. Davis, Mr. Wm. B. Floyd of York District, S. C., to Miss Margaret Johnson, of Gaston County, N. C.

Issue of May 15, 1852

Died Near Brattonsville, York District, on the 9th instant, Samuel Moore, in the 60th year of his age.
In Mississippi, on the 10th ultimo, Reverend Robert B. Walker, formerly of this District, in the 80th year of his age.

Issue of May 22, 1852

Married in Gaston County, N. C., on Tuesday the 11th inst., by Rev. Mr. O'Daniel, Mr. James Janes, of York District, S. C., to Miss Catharine, eldest daughter of John Massey, of the former place.
Died in this District on Sunday Morning last, Mr. Charles H. Sandifer, in the 24th year of his age.

Issue of May 29, 1852

Married on Sunday last 23d inst., by Rev. J. M. H. Adams, Mr. James M. Roach to Miss Sarah Elizabeth, second daughter of Mr. E. W. Smith, all of this District.
Departed this life on the 16th of May, at the residence of his father, Charles H. Sandifer, son of Philip & Sarah Sandifer of this District, in the 24th year of his age. (eulogy).

Issue of June 12, 1852

Died in this place on Sunday the 6th instant, Fannie Chambers, only daughter of John S. and Mariah J. Sadler, aged 4 months and 26 days.

Issue of June 19, 1852

Married at Chesterville on Wednesday the 16th inst., by Rev. S. L. Watson, J. L. M. Adams, Esq., of York District, to Miss Eliza, daughter of the late Robert Robinson, of the former place.

Issue of June 26, 1852

Died at the age of 73 at his residence in Bethel on the 21st inst., Mr. Samuel McCully, after a lingering illness...a member of the Presbyterian Church. (eulogy).

Issue of July 3, 1852

Died in this District after a short illness, on 2nd inst., Mr. William S. Sadler, aged about 28 years.

Issue of July 31, 1852

Married in this district on the 22d instant, by the Rev. S. L. Watson, Mr. John H. Boyd to Miss Jane A., daughter of John Laney, Esq.

Issue of August 7, 1852

Married on Thursday morning, 5th inst.,by the Rev. E. J. Meynardie, Mr. Jefferson Cline to Mrs. Sarah McKoy, all of this place.

On the 29th July, by Rev. S. L. Watson, Mr. John F. Glenn, to Miss Christiana C. Wood.

On the 20th ult., by Rev. Thomas Dickson, Mr. Thomas Mullinax to Miss Julia Ann Moore, all of this district.

On the 24th ult., by the Rev. Wade Hill, Mr. Henry Hulender to Miss Lethia Weare, all of this district.

Issue of August 15, 1852

Married on Thursday the 5th inst., by Rev. W. W. Rollins, John R. Shurley of Fairfield District, to Miss Mary Ann, third daughter of Alex. Fewell, Esq., of Ebenezerville, York District.

Issue of August 21, 1852

Married on Sunday morning the 15th instant, by Jas. Jefferys, Esq., Mr. Merrit Whitt, of Limestone Springs, Spartanburgh District, to Miss Ann Kelly, of this place.

On the 17th inst., by Rev. Mr. Farrer, Mr. William S. Baird to Miss Dianna Moore.

On the 19th instant, by Joseph McCosh, Esq., Mr. S. P. Pasour to Miss Dianah Broom, all of York District.

Died at Newton, Catawba County, North Carolina, August 3rd, Caleb L. Stowe, son of Abram and Elizabeth L. Stowe, in the 18th year of his age. This young man entered the Preparatory Department of Catawba College, located at Newton, N. C. at the commencement of the present session....member of the Presbyterian Church.

Issue of September 4, 1852

Married at the residence of Elins Mitchell, on Sunday, the 26th ult., by John Davis, Esq., Mr. James Briant to Miss Winney Cranford--both of York District.

On Thursday morning last,by the Rev. A. W. Miller, Mr. T. S. Fayssoux and Miss Melindy, eldest daughter of Isaac McFadden, of Chester District.

Died in Columbia, S. C., on Wednesday, 25th August ult., after a long illness, Mr. Robert Latta, aged 69 years.

YORKVILLE MISCELLANY

Issue of September 11, 1852

Died in Conway County, Arkansas, on the 11th of August, after
an illness of eight weeks, Mrs. Elizabeth G. Thomasson, consort
of P. A. Thomasson.

Issue of September 25, 1852

Married on the 14th inst., at Dr. W. A. Ardy's, Mecklenburg
County, N. C., by the Rev. W. C. Patterson, Mr. T. G. Culp, of
Lancaster District, S. C. to Miss Catharine McCallum of North
Carolina.

Issue of October 2, 1852

Died at the Moultrie House, Sullivan's Island at half-past
4 o'clock, on the 23d inst., Mr. T. W. Kennedy, of the firm of
O'Neale, Hill and Kennedy, of this city, aged about 33 years.
Mr. Kennedy had but a few months since removed from Columbia to
this city.... Charleston Mercury.

Issue of October 9, 1852

Married on the 23d ult., by A. Hardin, Esq., Mr. Philip
Ettress to Miss Elizabeth Dover, all of this District.
On the 22d ult.,by the Rev. Wm. Kerr, E. T. McKeown, of
Chester District to Miss Sarah H. Hoffman, of North Carolina,
Gaston County.
On Thursday the 30th ult., by the Rev. S. C. Hinton, Mr.
George S. Latimore, late of York District, to Miss Mary S., eldest
daughter of Mrs. N. Hudson of Chesterville.
Departed this life at Walterboro', S. C., on the night of
the 23d ult., of severe attack of Colic, Thomas Warren, formerly
a resident of this District in the 53d year of his age.

Issue of October 23, 1852

Married in Lowndes county, Miss., on the 23d September last
by the Rev. Samuel D. Johnson, Mr. J. Monroe Egger (son of Hugh
and Mary Egger) to Miss Emily, daughter of Alexander Morris,
formerly of York District.
Died, near Yorkville, on the 17th inst., Martha, daughter of
Rosanna and the late Jeremiah O'Leary, aged five years, two months
and twenty-nine days.
Of Consumption, at the residence of her father, in Lowndes
County, Miss., on the 3d of Sept last, Mrs. Polly Henry, wife of
John Henry, and daughter of Samuel Davis, and granddaughter of
Rev. Wm. C. Davis, of York Dist., Dec'd.

Issue of October 30, 1852

Death of Daniel Webster with account.
Died on Tuesday morning last,Mr. James Robeson, aged about 77 years.
The deceased was a native of Ireland, came to the United States
early in life, and resided, if correctly informed, the greater
part of his life in this District, and at the spot where he died.
(eulogy).
On Allison's creek, on Thursday night last, Mrs. Polly Turner
(at an advanced age), consort of George Turner.
In Walterboro', after a most protracted illness of eight

months, Mrs. Ann M. Warren, consort of the late Thomas Warren, formerly a resident near Yorkville.

Issue of November 6, 1852

Married at Nation Ford, York District, on the 20th ult., by the Rev. A. Whyte, Col. J. Brown Lewis, of Chester, to Margaret Jane, only daughter of the Rev. A.Whyte, of the former place.

Issue of November 13, 1852

Married on Sunday 21st of October by Ezekiel Fewel, Esq., Mr. Alexander Timberlake of this District, and Miss Elizabeth Buchanan of Gaston county.
On Tuesady the 2d inst., by Ezekiel Fewell, Esq., Mr. Wm. Forbess, and Miss Terrissa E. Wallace, all of this District.

Issue of December 5, 1852

Married on Thursday the 25th instant, by Moses McKeown, Esq., Mr. William H. Traylor of York District to Miss Isabella, daughter of Mr. William Miller, of Chester District.
Died at Charlotte, N. C., on the 24th instant, after a long protracted illness, Mr. Elijah G. Morris, aged about 46 years.

Issue of December 11, 1852

Married on Thursday the 18th November by Joseph M'Cosh, Esq., Mr. George Miller to Mrs. S. E. Grigg, all of this District.
On the 2d inst., by Rev. P.E. Bishop, Mr. G. W. Barris, to Miss Sarah J. Morris, all of this District.

Issue of December 23, 1852

Married on Tuesday 14th inst., by Rev. S. L. Watson, Mr. Duncan A. McCallum, Jr., to Miss Jane M. Wood, all of this District.
Near Yorkville on Tuesday, 21st inst., by Jas. Jefferys, esq., Mr. Stanford Camp of North Carolina, to Miss Sarah Jane Johnson, of this District.

Issue of January 8, 1853

Married on the evening of the 4th inst., by the Rev. R. Y. Russell, John L. Miller, Esq., to Miss Mary, daughter of S. Sadler, Esq., all of Yorkville.
Died at his residence in Gaston county, N. C.,on Tuesday, the 21st of December last, Rev. Joseph O'Daniel, a Minister of the Independent Presbyterian Church.
Died of Billious Remittent Fever, Oct. 25th, at the residence of John Brown, Esq., in Montgomery County, Illinois, Salmon S. Miles, after a protracted illness of four weeks.

Issue of January 15, 1853

Died in this village on Sunday night last, Mr. Jas. M. Byars, in the 22d year of his age.

Issue of January 22, 1853

Married on Thursday last, 20th inst., by Ezekiel Fewell, Esq.,

Mr. Thomas Huddleson, to Miss Mary Youngblood, all of this District.

Issue of January 27, 1853

Married on Thursday last,20th inst., by Rev. Samuel L. Watson, Mr. Jerome B. Brian, to Miss Mary C., daughter of the late Dr. J. B. Hunter, all of this District.
Died at the residence of his mother in this District on Thursday last, 20th inst., Mr. Andrew B. Simril, formerly of Yorkville, in the 34th year of his age.

Issue of February 3, 1853

Died in this District on the 29th January, Mr. John McDaniel, aged about 18 years.

Issue of February 10, 1853

Married on the 2d instant, by J. L. M. Adams, Esq., Mr. William Brannon to Miss Margaret Wallis, all of this District.

Issue of February 24, 1853

Married in this place, on Wednesday 16th inst., by Rev. William Boone, Mr. Joshua A. Stewart, of Burke County, N. Carolina, to Miss Lucinda, daughter of Mr. Samuel McCants.
Died in this village, on Friday, the 18th inst., of pulmonary affection, Mrs. Margaret L. McCorkle, wife of William H. McCorkle, and daughter of the late Robert Robinson, of Chesterville, aged 31 years and 7 days. (eulogy).
In this district on the 17th inst., Mr. Robert Mitchell Love, in the 53d year of his age.

Issue of March 3, 1853

Married in this District on Sunday last, by James Jefferys, Esq., Mr. James A. Scott, to Miss Rachel Louisa, eldest daughter of Mr. James and Sarah Kuykendal, all of this district.
Died in this place on Wednesday, 23d ult., Lucy Ann, youngest daughter of George S. and Alcester Doster, aged 8 months and 17 days.
In York District on the 12th ult., after a lingering illness, Mrs. Sarah, consort of Dr. G. W. Campbell, aged about 30 years.
On the 11th ult., at the residence of his brother, W. W. Carothers, in York District, John Ross, youngest son of J. & R. R. Carothers, in the 17th year of his age.

Issue of March 10, 1853

Married on Thursday last, 3d inst., by Rev. Mr. Garrison, Mr. George Milling, to Miss Ann Faris, all of this District.
Died at his own residence (York District, S. C.), on the 17th of February, Mr. R. M. Love, after a very short and sudden illness...a member of the Presbyterian Church, and for many years a Ruling Elder...a bereaved family, of which he was the sole surviving parent. (eulogy).

Issue of March 24, 1853

Died in this District on the 23d inst., Mr. S.Milton Jackson, in the 24th year of his age.

Issue of April 7, 1853

Married on Tuesday morning last, 5th inst., by Rev. Mr. Boon, Mr. Samuel W. Jackson, to Miss Rebecca, daughter of James Jefferys, Esq., all of this place.

In this village on Wednesday morning last, by Rev. J. M. H. Adams, Rev. James E. Morrison, of Concord, South Carolina, to Mrs. Julia L. Coulter of this District.

Issue of April 14, 1853

Married on the 6th instant, by the Rev. Mr. Murchison, Mr. Daniel F. Kelly, and Miss M. A. Altee, both of Columbia.

Died in this District on Saturday night last, 9th inst., after a short illness, Mr. Mansfield Gordon, in the 74th year of his age.

Issue of April 21, 1853

Died in this District on the 16th ult.,Mrs. Elizabeth J., wife of Capt. John Massey, in the 47th year of her age.

Issue of April 28, 1853

Married on Tuesday, 26th inst., by Rev. W. W. Carothers, Maj. John R. Wallace, to Miss Clementine L., daughter of Capt. Isaac Campbell, all of this District.

In this town on Sunday morning last, 24th inst., after a short illness, Mr. Newton W. Fewell, in the 33d year of his age.

In this district on Friday the 22nd inst., Mrs. Jane MCCleave, consort of Mr. Moses McCleave, in the 62d year of her age.

At his residence in Union District, after several weeks of painful suffering, on the morning of the 11th inst., Maj. William Giles in the 52d year of his age.

Issue of May 5, 1853

Died in this District on the 13th of April last, Mr. Brittou Bolin, in the 73d year of his age. Where the deceased was born, we are not informed. We only know from some of the oldest citizens of our village, that they have known Mr. Bolin, as a citizen of York District from their earliest recollection. The deceased was remarkable for his personal strength...sent to the defence of Charleston in the fall of 1814...reared up and leaves among us a large family.

Issue of May 12, 1853

Married on Tuesday morning, April 26th, by the Rev. Benjamin H. Evans, of St. George's Chapel, Beekman-street, New-York, Joseph A. Scoville, Editor of the New-York Pick, to Caroline, eldest daughter of Henry Schaub, Esq., of St. John's Berkley, South-Carolina.

Died in this place on Thursday morning last, Miss Harriet, third daughter of Stanhope and Mary A. Sadler, in the 17th year of her age.

Issue of May 19, 1853

Died in this District on Sunday morning last, Mr. Nathaniel
P. Kennedy, aged about 65 years.
In Madison county, Miss., on the 5th inst., Mr. W. D. Henry
formerly Sheriff of York District, aged about 63 years.
In this district on Thursday last, 12th inst., Mrs. Georgiana,
consort of F. M. Galbraith.
In this district on Friday, the 13th inst., Miss Mary Eliza
Riddle, in the 26th year of her age.

Issue of May 26, 1853

Died in this place on Thursday last, Mrs. Jane D. Moore, consort of Dr. William Moore.

Issue of June 2, 1853

Married near this place on Sunday the 29th ult., by James
Jefferys, Esq., Mr. Charles Pearson, of North Carolina, to Miss
Mary A. Murphy, of this District.

Issue of June 9, 1853

Married on Thursday the 2d inst., by Ezekiel Fewell, Esq.,
Mr. Charles McIlwain, and Miss Violet Jane, daughter of James
McCallum, all of this District.
Died in this District on Thursday 2d inst., Mr. Joshua Hudson,
in the 58th year of his age.
Of consumption, at the residence of the Rev. Silas J. Feemster,
in Lowndes County, Miss., on the 15th of May, ult., Mr. Samuel
Davis, son of the late Rev. William C. Davis, of York District,
S. C.
On the 25th of May, at his residence in Chester District,
Rev. James Loury, in the 74th year of his age.

Issue of June 16, 1853

Married in this place on the 8th inst., by Rev. J. M. H.
Adams, Mr. Walker B. Metts, of Laurens District, to Miss M.
Amanda, daughter of the late Andrew M'Connell, of this District.
Departed this life in this District on the 13th instant, Maj.
Thomas C. Black, in the 27th year of his age. (eulogy).

Issue of June 22, 1853

Married in this District on the 16th inst., by Rev. S. L. Wat-
son, Mr. Jas. T. Warren, to Miss Margaret R. Matthews, all of
this district.
Died at his residence in Bethel on the 8th inst., Mr. James
McCully, in the 77th year of his age...member of the Presbyterian
Church from his youth.
In this District on Tuesday morning last, 21st instant, Mr.
Robert Clinton, aged 24 years.

YORKVILLE MISCELLANY

Issue of June 29, 1853

Married in this District on the 23d inst., by Ezekiel Fewell, Esq., Mr. Joseph Absher to Miss Lucinda C. Kerr, all of this district.

Died in this District on Thursday last, 22d instant, Mr. Robert Fewell, aged about 55 years.

Issue of July 6, 1853

Married on Thursday evening 30th June at the Methodist Parsonage, in Columbia, by the Rev. Colin Murchison, W. A. Latta, Esq., of Yorkville, S. C., to Miss Sarah F. Dews, of the same place.

Died on the 1st instant, in this district, Mr. John U. McElmoyle, aged about 33 years.

Issue of July 20, 1853

Married at Talofa, Union District, on the 12th inst., by the Rev. Jas. M. H. Adams, Col. Samuel L. McConnell, of Yorkville, and Miss Mary C. Hoey, of the former place.

Died in this place on Friday the 15th inst., Mr. Edward C. McClain, aged about 43 years.

In Charlotte, N. C., on Friday the 15th inst., after an illness of four days, Mary William, infant daughter of James A. and Jane H. Sadler, aged 11 months and 25 days.

Issue of July 27, 1853

Married in this District, on Wednesday the 20th inst., by Ezekiel Fewell, Esq., Mr. John Garrison and Miss Mary, eldest daughter of Mr. Jonathan M. Neely, all of this district.

Died in this District on the 14th inst., Eliza Elanora, only daughter of Mr. R. Leroy and Mary A. Adams, aged one year, three months and one day.

Issue of August 3, 1853

Died in this district on Friday last,29th ult., Mrs. Mary Saville, aged about 75 years.

In this district near Fort Mill, on Sunday last, 31st ult., Mr. ___ Streeter, aged about 35 years.

In Asheville, N. C., on the 23d ultimo, in the 30th year of her age, Mrs. Mary Catharine, wife of Mr. D. A. Gordon, of this place.

Issue of August 10, 1853

Died suddenly in this place, on Saturday morning, 6th inst., Charlie, third son of W. I. and M. J. Clawson, aged 1 years and 10 months.

In this District, at the residence of his brother, on the 21st ult., Mr. A. N. Hall, in the 35th year of his age...a native of this district, but for more than two years a resident of Florida...left a wife and two children.....

In Coosa county, Alabama, on the 22d ultimo, Mrs. Elizabeth Parish, aged about 75 years, consort of Mr. Isaac Parish formerly of this District, for the last 14 years a resident of Alabama.

Issue of August 31, 1853

Died in this district, on the 26th inst., Miss Martha Ann, daughter of Mr. Robert Lindsey, in the 16th year of her age.

On the 11th inst., in Cleaveland county, N. C., near Shelby, Mr. Aaron Beam, in the fifty first year of his age...left a wife and six children(eulogy).

Issue of September 7, 1853

Married on the 23d ult., by Ezekiel Fewell, Esq., Mr. Henry Reaves, to Miss Harriet Adkins, all of this District.

On the 4th inst., by Ezekiel Fewell, Esq., Mr. Abram P. Hagins, to Miss Martha E. Hagins, all of this district.

Issue of September 14, 1853

Died in this place on Wednesday evening, 7th inst., Mary Lucinda, daughter of Mr. James A. Estes, aged about 18 months.

In this district on Sunday night, 11th instant, Mr. David S. Patton, aged about 60 years.

In this district, on Saturday the 3d inst., Mr. John Richardson, in the 25th year of his age.

In this district on Monday the 12th instant, Mr. Benjamin Warren, aged 83 years.

Issue of September 21, 1853

Death of Col. S. L. M'Connell...died at his residence in this place on Monday morning last...

Issue of September 28, 1853

Died in Yorkville, S. C.,on the morning of the 18th instant, Mr. Samuel L. McConnel, aged 31 years...a native of York District, and in early years was employed as a clerk in the house of Wood, Beatty, & Co. (long eulogy).

Died in Yorkville, on the 26th instant, Dr. John Ratchford, a native of this District, aged 31 years. He was a graduate of the S. C. College, after which he studied medicine and received his diploma from Castleton College, Vermont...a member of the Independent Presbyterian Church...left a widow, aged parents, brothers and sisters.

Died in this District, on the 18th inst., William Glenn, Esq., aged about 60 years.

In this District on the 32d(sic) instant, Mr. Samuel Wilson, aged about 40 years.

Issue of October 5, 1853

Married on Tuesday evening 27th ult., by Rev. P. E. Bishop, Mr. John J. Jones, to Miss Jane, youngest daughter of the late William Steedman, all of this District.

Died in this District on the 2nd instant, Edward H. Gunning, formerly of the firm of Steele, Gunning & Co., aged about 38 years...(eulogy).

Died, in this District,on the 1st instant, John S., son of Alexander and Luvisa Stewart, aged four years and six months.

Issue of October 12, 1853

Married in the vicinity of Ebenezer, on the 4th inst., at the residence of Madison Neely, Esq.,by the Rev. J. Monroe Anderson, Mr. W. D. Philips, of Wadesborough, N. C. to Miss Dorcas Catharine Powell, of this District.

In this District on the 24th ult., Mrs. Mary Faris, aged 87 years.

At the residence of his father in this District, on the 30th September, William Wilson Galbraith, aged 7 years, 4 months and 10 days.

Issue of October 19, 1853

Died in this District on Thursday the 13th instant, Elizabeth Catherine, daughter of Alexander and Luvisa Stewart, aged two years and one day.

In this district, on Thursday the 13th instant, Jacob S., son of Benjamin S. and Paulina Fox, aged six months.

Issue of October 26, 1853

Married in Chester District on Wednesday, 19th inst., by the Rev. Miller, Dr. Wm. C. D. Melton, formerly of Yorkville, to Miss Mary Jane, daughter of John Poag, esq., of the former place.

Died in this district, on the 19th inst., Mr. James Harper, aged about 60 years. Mr. H. was a good citizen, an obliging neighbor and an affectionate parent. He has left a wife and three children....

Issue of December 21, 1853

Married in Dallas, N. C., on the 12th inst., by W. M. Holland, Mr. J. G. Schorb, of Winnsboro, S. C., and Miss Mary Ann Ivens, of Gaston County, N. C.

Issue of January 18, 1854

Married on Thursday the 12th inst., by Thomas J. Eccles, Esq., Mr. James Garvin and Miss Salanthia C. Pollard, all of York District.

On Thursday the 12th inst., by Rev. Samuel L. Watson, Mr. G. W. Flanigan, to Miss Rebecca Caroline Adams, all of this district.

Died in this district on the 30th ult., Mr. Alexander Sutton, aged about 65 years.

Issue of January 7, 1853 (Vol. 2, #9)

Married on the evening of the 4th inst., by the Rev. R. Y.
Russell, John L. Miller, Esq., Commissioner in Equity of York,
to Miss Mary, daughter of S. Sadler, Esq., all of Yorkville.

In Gaston county (N. C.), on the 28th ult., by Rev. Mr.
Suttle, Mr. Charles Q. Petty of Spartanburg, S. C., to Miss Sarah
Jane Cobb, of the former place.

Died at his residence in Gaston county, N. C., on Tuesday,
____ (torn), Rev. Joseph O'Daniel, minister of the Independent
Presbyterian Church. Mr. O'Daniel was born in this District, on
the 28th of February 1808...(long account and eulogy).

Issue of October 12, 1853

Married in the vicinity of Ebenezer, on the 4th inst., at the
residence of F. Madison Neely, Esq., by the Rev. J. M. Anderson,
Mr. W. D. Phillips of Wadesborough, N. C. to Miss Dorcas Catharine
Powell, of this District.

Died, in this district, on the 30th ult., at the residence
of his father, F. M. Galbraith, William Wilson Galbraith, aged
seven years, four months and nineteen days.

Died at the residence of his son in this District, on Tuesday
the 27th ult., Mr. Joseph Jamieson, a soldier of the Revolution,
in the 89th year of his age. His mother had been widowed by the
death of his father, some years before the separation of the
colonies from the mother country, and was left to depend upon
the energy and industry of her two sons, James and Joseph for the
support of herself and her orphan children....(long account)...
guarded the log meeting house of Bullock's Creek Church, while
the Rev. Dr. Joseph Alexander, preached the gospel to his people....

Issue of April 5, 1855 (Vol. I, #13)

We sincerely regret to learn the particulars of a sad event
which occurred in Chester District on Friday last, and resulted
in the death of a slave Andrew, the property of Mr. Richard E.
Kennedy, at the hands of a young man named Bell. The boy, who
had been hired by Mr. Bell as a laborer on his farm, ran away
several weeks ago and remained in the woods until Friday, when
he was caught and whipped so severely and unmercifully as to
cause immediate death....

Died March 6th, 1855, in Lowndesboro', Ala., Major John G.
Rogers. He was born in Lancaster District, South Carolina, 12th
July 1817. He left a widow and four children and a large number
of friends to mourn his loss...once filled the office of Census-
Taker in Lowndes County...the old gentleman was of the Seceder
persuasion...funeral discourse by Rev. J. M. Jennings. (eulogy)
Lowndes County Chronicle

Died in this District, on the 31st ult., Mr. Jas. Johnston,
in the 75th year of his age.

Issue of April 12, 1855

Married in this District, on Tuesday the 3d instant, by Rev.
S. L. Watson, Mr. Hugh Tate, and Miss Mary Carothers.

Issue of April 26, 1855

Died of Consumption at his father's residence in Fairfield
District, on Saturday, 7th inst., Mr. James Gregg Leitner, in the
24th year of his age. (tribute of respect).

Married on Sunday morning the 15th inst., at the residence
of Mr. Wat Anderson, son of the groom, by the Rev. H. W. Ledbetter,
Mr. Richard Anderson, aged seventy-six, to Miss Sally McKelden,
aged twenty, all of Abbeville district.

Died Suddenly at Troy, New York, Female Seminary, of the
disease of the heart, Miss Harriet Sidney, daughter of the late
Benjamin and Mrs. Eliza A. Neely, aged about 16 years.

In this District, on Saturday the 24th inst., Mr. William
Sandlin, aged about 21 years.

Issue of May 10, 1855

Married in this District on the 26th ult.,by Rev. R. A. Ross,
Mr. William W. Cain, and Miss Jane, daughter of Mr. Henry Wallace.

In this place on Wednesday morning, the 9th inst., by Rev. J.
M. H. Adams, Hon. Daniel Wallace, of Jonesville, Union District,
and Mrs. Emily H. Starr, of Yorkville.

In this District, on the 3d instant, by Thomas J. Bell, esq.,
Mr. Daniel E. Seehorn, and Miss Mary S., eldest daughter of Capt.
J. W. A. Hartness.

In Rowan County, North Carolina, on the 25th ult.,by Rev.
J. B. O. Wilson, Mr. Robert F. Hall of this District, and Miss
Mary E. Hall.

At Unionville, on the 1st instant, by Rev. J. H. Saye, Giles
J. Patterson, esq., of Chester, and Miss M. J. Gage, of the
former place.

On Thursday the 3d inst., by Rev. P. E. Bishop, Mr. William
Bennett and Miss Martha, daughter of Clark Robinson, all of this
district.

In this District, on Thursday the 3d instant, by Ezekiel

Fewell, Esq., Mr. John C.Armer, of Dallas County, North Carolina,
aged 53 years to Mrs. Sarah McCain, aged 69.
  Died in this District at the residence of Mr. Henry Wallace,
on Saturday the 28th ult., Elvira Jane, only child of Mr. Robert
Latham, aged about two years.

Issue of May 17, 1855

  Died in this place on Sunday morning last, Mrs. Mary Darwin,
wife of Peyton B. Darwin, Esq., aged about 50 years.
  In Charlotte, N. C., on the 8th inst., of puerperal fever,
Mrs. Octavia Jones, wife of E. P. Jones, Esq., and daughter of
John Irwin, Esq., aged about 28 years.
  At South Point, Gaston County, N. C.,on the 16th ult., Mrs.
Mary A. A. Craig, wife of Mr. Samuel W. Craig, and daughter of
James A. Henderson, Esq., in the 24th year of her age.

Issue of May 24, 1855

  Married at Hood's Factory, in this District, by J. P. Hood,
Esq., Mr. James Petty and Miss Mary Rhey, all of this District.
  Died in this District on Wednesday the 16th instant, after a
short illness, Mr. James E. Wham, aged about 23 years.
  In this District, on Saturday evening last, of Typhus Fever,
Mrs. Sophia Howell, wife of Mr. Williamson Howell, aged about 63
years.

Issue of August 9, 1855

  Married in this place on Tuesday morning the 7th instant,
by Rev. G. W. M. Craighton, Mr. Wesley Creps, and Miss Harriet,
daughter of Mrs. James, all of this place.
  On Thursday last, 24 instant, by Rev. R. A. Ross, Mr. Samuel
T. Patrick, and Miss Henrietta Gwinn, all of this District.

Issue of August 30, 1855

  Married in this District on the 15th instant, by Rev. J. R.
Baird, Mr. Thomas P. Whisonant and Miss Mary Jane Hambright, all
of this district.
  Died in Yorkville, on Sunday the 26th instant, Mrs. Maria
Goore, widow of Capt. Joshua D. Goore, in the 53d year of her age.
Mrs. Goore was a native of New-York, but for a long term of
years her residence has been in our midst...(eulogy)
  On the morning of the 28th instant, was deposited in the Ceme-
tery of the Independent Presbyterian Church, Yorkville, S. C., the
remains of an infant son of Mary and Richard Hare....
  Died of inflamation of the bowels, in Fayette County, Tenn.,
on the 16th instant, Mrs. Sarah P., wife of J. H. Garrison, leaving
two infant children to mourn her loss.

Issue of September 20, 1855 [issue at UNC, Chapel Hill]

  Died in Yorkville, on Wednesday evening, 12th instant, Mr.
Valdewra Josiah Sylvester Smith, eldest son of Maj. Myles Smith,
aged 24 years and 7 months.
  In this District on Tuesday 11th instant, Mrs. Nancy H. Mc-
Elwee, consort of Mr. James McElwee, in the 53d year of her age.
  In Ebenezerville, York District, Minnie, daughter and only
child of E. T. and Mary Avery, about one year of age.

YORKVILLE ENQUIRER

Issue of October 25, 1855

Married in York District, on the 14th inst., by Ezekiel
Fewell, Esq., Mr. J. B. Smith, and Miss R. J. Ford, all of Gaston
Co., N. C.

Issue of November 1, 1855

Married on Tuesday, the 30th instant, by Jas. Jefferys, Esq.,
Joseph W. Aiken and Mary Aiken, all of this District.

Issue of November 22, 1855

Married on the 18th instant, by Thos. J. Eccles, Esq., Mr.
Robert W. Gardner and Miss Mary Turner, all of York District.
Died in this District on Saturday the 17th instant, Julia
Richardson, infant daughter of A. B. Springs, Esq., aged 10 months.
Died on the first day of November, Mary H., infant daughter of
James G. and Jane E. Love, aged two years.

Issue of November 29, 1855

Married by Joseph McCosh, Esq., on the 25th instant, Mr.
William Foster and Miss Adaline Page, both of Union District,
S. C.

Issue of December 6, 1855

Married by Rev. S. L. Watson, on the 29th of November, Mr. James
A. Jackson, and Miss Mary L. C. Hemphill, all of this District.
Died in this District on the 27th ultimo, Samuel Parks, eldest
son of Wm. M. and Sarah D. Watson, aged 6 years and two months....

Issue of December 20, 1855

Married on the 11th inst., by Rev. J. R. Baird, Mr. M. Garri-
son, and Miss Sarah A. Hutchison, all of this District.
And on the 13th instant, by Rev. J. R. Baird, Mr. N. A. Steele,
and Mrs. E. R. Watson, all of this District.
At Spartanburg, C. H., on the 11th inst., by Rev. John D.
McCullough, Edward Moore, Esq., of Yorkville, and Miss Phoebe
D. Wheeler, of the former place.
On Tuesday the 11th instant, at the residence of the bride's
father, by Rev. R. K. Porter, Rev. David H. Porter, Pastor of the
First Presbyterian Church, Savannah, and Miss Mary Birney, youngest
daughter of Mr. Samuel Clarke, of Beech Island.

Issue of January 3, 1856

Married in Ripley, Miss., by ____, Mr. Samuel Graham, formerly
of York District, to Mrs. Harriet Porter, of the former place.
On the 1st instant, by Rev. W. C. Owen, Mr. Warren Lynn, and
Miss Betsey White, all of this District.

Issue of January 24, 1856

Married in this District, on Wednesday the 16th instant, by
Rev. J. R. Baird, Mr. James F. Hutchison, and Miss Mary Ann Faries.
In this district on Thursday the 17th instant, by A. S. Wal-
lace, esq., Mr. James Acock and Miss Mary E. McCallum.

Married in Yorkville on Wednesday morning, the 23d instant, by Rev. J. Monroe Anderson, Dr. John W. Simpson of Laurens to Mrs. Jane C. Clowney of Union District.

Died in this District on the 17th instant, Miss Mary Elizabeth, eldest daughter of D. F. And Sarah R. Jackson, in the 18th year of her age....

Issue of January 31, 1856

Married on the 24th inst., at Live Oak, Richland District, by Rev. J. L. Reynolds, D. D., J. Hampden Brooks, of Edgefield to Mary Goodwyn, eldest daughter of Gov. Jas. H. Adams.

In Charleston, on the 23d inst., at the residence of Capt. G. Fellin, by the Rev. Dr. Corcoran, M. W. Bythewood, of this city, to Miss G. M. Kittleband, of Charleston.

At Abbeville, S. C., on 1st instant, by Rev. B. Johnson, William Henry Parker to Lucia G., daughter of Hon. D. L. Wardlaw, all of that place.

Issue of February 14, 1856

Married on Thursday the 7th instant, by William McGill, Esq., Mr. John Patterson, of North Carolina, to Miss Elizabeth, daughter of R. M. Faries of this District.

Died in this District, near Bethel Church, Mr. Robert Campbell, aged eighty years.

Issue of February 21, 1856

Married on Tuesday evening the 8th ultimo, by J. R. Logan, Esq., Mr. T. G. Borders and Miss Susan Martha Logan, all of Cleveland County, N. C.

On Wednesday, the 13th inst., by J. R. Logan, Esq., Mr. John W. Murray of Rutherford County, to Miss Sophia Emiline Beatty, of Cleaveland County, N. C.

In this District on Tuesday the 12th instant, by Rev. R. Y. Russell, Mr. Robert T. H. Smith and Miss Jane, daughter of Mr. Elias Jackson.

Died on the 15th instant of Croup, Little Charlie, only son of T. S. & M. A. Jefferys, aged 1 year 2 months and 25 days.

Issue of February 28, 1856

Married in Chester, on the 18th instant, by Rev. J. L. Pritchard, Dr. G. J. Hinton, and Miss Eliza Jane, daughter of Maj. Jno. Kennedy.

On Thursday the 14th inst.,by Rev. Samuel L. Watson, Mr. Wm. H. Johnson, of Gaston Co., N. C. to Miss Zereriah McGill of this District.

On Thursday 21st instant, by Rev. J. R. Baird, Mr. Hugh F. Ewing, of Gaston Co., N. C. to Miss Mary E. Garrison, of York District.

On the 13th instant, by the Rev. David Wills, Col. John D. Williams, of Laurens District, to Miss Ann Eliza Barnett, of Abbeville District.

Died at the residence of her father, Alexander Anderson, of Marshal Co., Miss., on the 15th of September last, Mrs. Eliza Jaggers, consort of Oliver Jaggers, aged about 55 years. She leaves a husband, four children and numerous friends to mourn her loss.

Issue of March 6, 1856

Married in this place on Tuesday last, by Rev. A. H. Lester, Peyton E. Darwin, Esq.,and Miss Jerusha James.

Died at his residence in this vicinity, on Tuesday last, of disease of the heart, Mr. George Ratchford, aged 81 years.

Issue of March 13, 1856

Married on Thursday, the 6th instant, by A. S. Wallace, Esq., Mr. William Clinton and Miss Sarah Jane Miskelly, all of this district.

Died in this Village on Tuesday the 4th instant, Annie Leigh, infant daughter of Chas. B. and Ann R. Knowles, aged 1 year, 6 months and 16 days.

On Wednesday the 5th inst., Mr. Hamilton Carroll, aged 73 years.

Issue of March 20, 1856

Died in this District on Saturday the 15th instant, Mr. Joseph Poag, aged about 60 years.

Issue of March 27, 1856

Married at Barttonsville, in this District, on Thursday evening the 20th instant, by Rev. J. E. White, Maj. T. J. Dunovant, of Chester, and Miss Jane, daughter of the late Dr. John S. Bartton.

Died in this District, on Saturday, the 15th instant, Miss Sarah Ann Floyd, in the 41st year of her age.

Issue of April 10, 1856

Died on the 2d day of April at Davidson College, N. C., William Morrison, infant son of Maj. D. R. & Mrs. J. M. Hill, aged 4½ months.

At his residence near Sandersville, Chester District, on the 14th of March ult., Capt. Jas. A. Gaston, of Dropsy, aged 56 years.

On the 24th ult., near Landsford, Chester District (at the residence of her son, L. A. Beckham), Mrs. Jane Beckham, in the 85th year of her age.

In Chester District, on the 27th ult., after a lingering illness, Mrs. Jane Gladden, wife of Lacey Gladden.

On the 27th ult., Miss Esther Gaston, of Chester District, in the 21st year of her age.

Issue of April 17, 1856

Married on Thursday the 10th inst.,by Rev. Mr. Robinson, Dr. Alfred Craven of Yorkville, and Miss Cornelia, daughter of Dr. J. F. G. Mittag, of Lancaster.

In Union District, on Thursday 10th inst., by Rev. W. W. Carothers, Mr. J. H. Garrison, of Spartanburg District, and Miss Milly W. McCulloch, of the former place.

Died in Union District, on the 30th ultimo, after an illness of ten days, Mrs. M. H. Parker, aged 43 years and one month. (long eulogy).

Died in this District on Friday the 4th instant, Mrs. Mary
Peters, relict of John Peters, aged about eighty-four years.

Issue of April 24, 1856

Married in Newberry Distirct, on Thursday the 17th instant,
Col. John S. Sitgreaves of York District, to Mrs. E. Suber, of
the former place.
Died in this place on Monday last, of Consumptino, Mrs. Catharine J., wife of John G. Enloe, Esq., aged about 34 years.

Issue of May 8, 1856

Married in this place on Tuesday morning, 6th instant, by
Rev. R. Y. Russell, Mr. Daniel O'Leary and Miss Ann R., daughter
of Thomas S. Pagan, Esq., all of Yorkville.
On the 10th ultimo, by Rev. L. C. Hinton, Mr. Richard Wilks,
and Miss Mary E. B., eldest daughter of Joseph T. Tims, all of
Chester District.
Departed this life on Monday morning, 28th ult., Mrs. Elvira
Jane, consort of Samuel J. Kuykendal, of this village, and daughter of Capt. John Chambers, deceased, of this district. Her
age was 38 years, 1 month and 10 days. (eulogy).
Died in this place on Monday the 21st ult., of Pulmonary disease, Mrs. Catharine J. Enloe, wife of John John G. Enloe, and
daughter of Mr. Hugh and Mrs. Violet Allison, in the 33d year of
her age...member of the A. R. Presbyterian Church at Tirzah in
the year 1844 under the preaching of Rev. L. McDonald...(long
eulogy).

Issue of May 15, 1856

Married on the 22d ult., by Joseph White, Esq.,Mr. John Alexander and Miss Mary Burns, all of this District.
Died in this District on the 5th instant, Mrs. Susannah, consort of Godfrey Beamguard, deceased, in the 65th year of her age.
In Chester District, on Tuesday the 6th instant, after a
short illness, Mr. James C. M. Brown, aged about 56 years.

Issue of May 22, 1856

Married on the 15th inst., by Rev. S. L. Watson, Mr. R. A.
Clinton, of Texas, and Miss Jane Brown of this District.
In Chester District, on Thursday the 1st of May, by Rev. L.
C. Hinton, Col. John R. Culp and Miss Fannie Ragsdale.
Died in Chesterville, on the 10th instant, Mrs. Phoebe Matilda
wife of Mr. Thomas DeGraffenreid, aged 39 years.

Issue of May 29, 1856

Married on Thursday the 22d inst., by Rev. E. E. Boyce, Mr.
R. B. Alexander and Miss Margaret E. Allison, all of this District.
On Thursday the 22d inst., by Rev. A. Whyte, Mr. William D.
Hagins, of York District, to Miss Lizzie K. Hough, formerly of
Lebanon, New Hampshire.

Issue of June 5, 1856

Married in This District on Tuesday the 27th ult.,by Rev.
R. A. Ross, R. E. Allison, Esq., and Miss Mary A., eldest daughter
of Mr. Ed. R. Chambers.

At Woodlawn, Columbia, on Thursday morning, May 29, by Rev.
R. M. Palmer, Rufus M. J. Johnston, of New York, and Ann Cecilia,
eldest daughter of the late Robert Latta.

In Edgefield District, on Tuesday the 27th ult., by the Rev.
Mr. Zimmerman, Cicero Adams, Esq., formerly of Lancaster, and
Miss Mary A., daughter of Maj. John Hughes, of Edgefield.

At Clarksville, Va., on Wednesday, the 28th ultimo, by Rev.
Mr. Naylor, Mr. J. E. Weikert, formerly of Pennsylvania, and Miss
Margaret A. Gregory, of the former place.

Issue of June 12, 1856

Died of typhoid pneumonia, on the morning of the 5th instant,
at the residence of Mr. William Verry, in this District, Mrs. Jane
Smarr, in the 63d year of her age...member of the Presbyterian
church. (long eulogy).

On Monday the 9th instant, at midnight, Mary A., eldest daughter of Dr. James M. and Louisa E. Lowry, in the 10th year of her
age....

Died after an illness of about four months, on Tuesday morning,
10th instant, Mrs. Frances, wife of B. Steele Carson, in the 49th
year of her age.

Issue of June 19, 1856

Married in this District, on Thursday the 12th instant, by
Rev. S. L. Watson, Mr. H. B. Hemphill and Miss M. C. Jackson.

On the 10th instant, by Rev. A. Whyte, Mr. R. S. Wilson, of
Charlotte, N. C. and Miss L. J. Patterson, of this District.

In Mecklenburg County, N. C., on the 10th instant, by the
Rev. John G. Richards, Mr. Thomas M. Carothers, of York District,
S. C., to Miss Levica Jane, eldest daughter of Major John M.
Potts, of the former place.

Also, on the 12th instant, by the Rev. John R. Pickett, Mr.
T. S. Riddle of Lancasterville, S. C., to Miss Sarah L., daughter
of Mr. Henry Marks, of Mecklenburg County.

Died in this District, on the 3d instant, Mr. James M. Spratt.

On the 29th ultimo, in this District, Mrs. Elizabeth, wife of
Mr. Thomas C. Traylor, aged about 40 years.

Issue of June 26, 1856

Died at his residence near Smith's Ford, Union District, on
the 18th instant, John W. Darwin, in the thirty-fourth year of
his age...a member of the Baptist denomination...(eulogy).

Died in Canton, Madison County, Mississippi, on the morning
of the 5th inst., Mrs. Margaret Henry, relict of the late Wm.
D. Henry, formerly of York District, and mother of Hon. E. G.
Henry. The deceased had reached her seventy-fifth year...(eulogy)
Canton Commonwealth.

Died at his residence in Chester District, on the 16th instant,
Mr. George W. Bell, in the 56th year of his age....

Issue of July 3, 1856

Death of Col. S. W. Trotti. We are pained to see the announce-
ment of the death of Col. Samuel Wilds Trotti, who died at the
residence of Mrs. F. Means, near Buckhead on the 24th inst. Col.
Trotti was born in Barnwell district, and educated at the South
Carolina College. He served the State in the Legislature and in
Congress....Carolinian.

Died in Lincolnton, N. C., on the 20th ultimo, William Williamson, aged 45 years... A Prominent lawyer and an accomplished gentleman. (eulogy. T. J. E.

In this place on the 23d ult., Mr. Samuel Carson, aged about
32 years.

On the 23d ultimo, at Bennettsville, Marlboro' District, S. C.,
at the House of Rev. P. E. Bishop, Miss MaryA. M. McKnight, after
an illness of fifteen days.

Issue of July 17, 1856

Married at Orangeburg, on the 3d instant, by Rev. B. M.
Palmer, Mr. Micah Jenkins of Yorkville, and Miss Caroline H.,
eldest daughter of Gen. D. F. Jamieson, of the former place.

Died in this District on Wednesday the 9th instant, Mr. William
Crawford, in the 76th year of his age.

Issue of July 24, 1856

Died in this place on Thursday, 17th instant, Willis Miller,
infant son of Lewis M. and Frances V. Grist, aged 4 months and
10 days.

On the 5th instant, near Horn Lake, DeSoto County, Miss., Mr.
J. Bishop McCorkle, in the 18th year of his age.

On the 25th of February last, in Scott County, Arkansas, Mr.
Robert Finley, formerly of this District, aged 46 years.

In the vicinity of Yorkville on the 20th inst., Julia Octavia
fourth daughter of Thomas and Paulina Wood, aged three years and
two months.

Issue of July 31, 1856

Married in Yorkville on the 24th instant, by Thomas J. Eccles,
Esq., Mr. J. D. Miskelly and Miss Nancy E. Land, all of York
District.

On the 22d inst., by the Rev. J. D. Gibson, Mr. John B. Pankey,
of York District and Miss Emma L. Johnson, of Chester District.

Died in Yorkville on the 24th inst., after a severe and
protracted illness, Nancy Isabella, second daughter of Abraham
Garvin, aged 11 years, 10 months and 8 days.

In this district at the residence of Allen Robinson, Esq., on
the 26th instant, Wm. Robinson, Esq., of Long Town, Fairfield
District, S. C., in the 83d year of his age.

In York District, of Flux, on the 6th instant, Miss Mary
Robinson, aged about 20 years. Also, on the 15th, Jonathan,
aged 3 years. Also, on the 24th, Mrs. Margaret Robinson, aged
45 years; the daughter, son and wife of Mr. Clark Robinson.

In Charleston, S. C., on the 23d inst., John A. Gyles, Esq.,
Attorney at Law, R. W. Grand Secretary of the Grand Lodge of
the I. O. O. F. of South Carolina....

Issue of August 7, 1856

Married on Thursday, 31st ultimo, by Rev. S. L. Watson, Mr. James R. Harper and Miss Pauline M. Turner, all of this District.

Died in this District on the 3d instant, Mary Rebecca, infant daughter of H. Lorraine and Jane M. Swann, aged 11 months and 12 days.

Issue of August 14, 1856

Died, in this place, on Sabbath, the 10th inst., after a very sever and protracted illness, Mrs. Janette Amelia, wife of I. D. Witherspoon, Jr., Esq....Just two weeks before, her babe had been called to the Saviour's bosom...(eulogy).

Died in Yorkville, on Saturday morning, 9th instant, Mr. F. L. Hoffman, in the 36th year of his age.

In this place on Sunday, 10th instant, after a short illness, George R. Williams, son of G. W. Williams, Esq., in the 20th year of his age.

In this place on Friday, the 8th inst., Leroy, only child of Franklin and Margaret Blankenship, aged about 14 months.

Issue of August 21, 1856

Married in this District on Thursday the 14th instant, by Rev. E. E. Boyce, Mr. A. P. Quinn, and Miss Jane E. Thomasson, all of this District.

In this District on the 14th instant, by Rev. E. E. Boyce, Mr. William Quinn and Miss Mary S. Brown, all of this District.

Died at the residence of his father, near Fort Mill, on Thursday, 14th instant, of Typhoid Fever, Mr. William G. Faulkner, in the 26th year of his age.

In Fayette County, Tennessee, on the 7th inst., Mr. Cardelia N. Pierce, formerly of York District, aged 64 years.

Issue of September 11, 1856

Married on Tuesday the 26th of August, by Rev. S. L. Watson, Mr. Josiah T. Davis, and Miss Sarah Hill, all of this District.

On Thursday the 4th instant, by Rev. Samuel L. Watson, Mr. William Jackson, and Miss Margaret Currence, all of this Distirct.

Issue of September 18, 1856

Married on Thursday the 11th instant, by A. Hardin, Esq., Mr. A. A. Hullender and Miss J. A. Johnson, all of this District.

Died in Gaston Co., N. C., on Sunday 24th of August, Thomas McLean, Sr., aged 92 years and 14 days.

Issue of September 25, 1856

Died at the residence of Rev. J. Monroe Anderson, in Yorkville, of Paralysis, on the 23d inst., Mrs. Sarah Starr, in the 80th year of her age.

Died in DeSoto County, Miss., on the 11th of August, 1856, Laura H., daughter of Moses M. and Sarah White, formerly of Lancaster District, S. C....

Mrs. Margaret Philadelphia Smith Porter departed this life on the morning of the 18th of September, 1856, aged 23 years and 7 days, of catarrhal fever, leaving a bereaved husband with two children...member of the M. E. Church....

Issue of October 2, 1856

Married in this District on the 23d instant, by Rev. James R. Castles, Mr. R. S. Berry, and Miss Elvie, daughter of Samuel Black.

Issue of October 9, 1856

Married on the 2d instant at the residence of F. M. Galbraith, Esq., by Rev. A. H. Lester, Mr. Z. J. Howell, of Chester, and Miss Amanda M. Galbraith, of York District.

In Yorkville, on Thursday, 24 instant, by Rev. J. M. H. Adams, Mr. James V. Ferguson, and Miss Jane A., third daughter of William R. & Emily E. Alexander, all of this District.

On the 30th ultimo, by A. S. Wallace, Esq., Mr. Daniel McElmoyle, and Miss Mary Pardue, all of this District.

On Tuesday, 23d ultimo, by Rev. Thomas Dickson, Mr. E. Blalock, and Miss M. E. Guntharp, all of this District.

On the 28th ultimo, by Joseph McCosh, Esq., Mr. Thomas Adkins and Miss Jane E. Starnes, all of York District.

Issue of October 16, 1856

Married near Buzzard Roost, on Thursday, 9th instant, by Rev. R. Y. Russell, Mr. Moses Latham and Miss Catharine McSwain, all of this District.

In Buzzard Roost, on Sunday morning, 12th instant, by J. P. Hood, Esq., Mr. Hicks McSwain and Miss Mary Ann Chambers, all of this district.

On the 1st instant, by Wm. McGill, Esq., Mr. H. H. Montgomery, and Catharine Clark, all of this District.

On the 9th instant, by Wm. McGill, Esq., Mr. James M. Dover, and Miss Amanda M. Nichols, all of this District.

Died on Friday, the 10th instant, of Flux, William Alexander, only son of James McSwain, aged 6 years and six months.

Issue of October 23, 1856

Died in this District on Saturday the 18th instant, of Dropsy, Mr. David McIlwain, in the 78th year of his age.

On the 15th inst., James Richards, son of Dr. J. A. Barnett, aged 15 months and 1 day.

It is only a few weeks since, we were called upon to record the death, from an injury received at the Railroad, of the eldest son of our friend, the Rev. Ferdinand Jacobs, of Charleston.... We refer to the death of his beloved wife, Annie R., which took place on Friday evening, the tenth of this month, in the 36th year of her life. The following tribute appears in the Southern Presbyterian:

Mrs. Jacobs was the eldest daughter of the late Genl. James W. Ripley, of Maine; and a great-grand-daughter of President Wheelock, the founder of Dartmouth College...(eulogy).

Issue of November 6, 1856

Married in Richland District on the 21st of October, by Rev. W. D. Beverly, Mr. Charles W. Rawlinson, and Miss M. Malinda, daughter of John Scott, Esq.

Died in this place on the 18th ultimo, William Sylvannus, only child of John S. and Mariah J. Sadler, aged 19 months.

On the 3d instant, Ringold, only child of Samuel E. and Anna C. Moore, aged 4 years and 9 months.

Issue of November 13, 1856

Married on the 6th inst., by Rev. Mr. Crook, Mr. C. B. Smith, of Smith's Turn Out, and Miss Sallie E. Harden, of Chester District.

Issue of November 20, 1856

Married in Yorkville, on Wednesday the 12th inst., by Rev. J. M. H. Adams, Mr. Thomas McLure Jr. of Chester, and Miss Jane E., daughter of the late Benjamin Neely, of this place.
In this district on the 18th instant, by Rev. J. M. Anderson, Mr. J. W. Steele and Miss Margaret W.,daughter of Rev. S. L. Watson.

Issue of December 4, 1856

Married in this District on the 2nd ult.,by A. Hardin, Esq., Mr. John H. Reives, and Miss Hannah E. Mullenax.
On the 11th ult., by A. Hardin, Esq., Mr. Martin L. Randall, and Miss Nancy C. Whisenant.
On the 23d ult.,by A. Hardin, Esq., Mr. James H. Hambright, and Miss Rebecca Biolet Holmes, eldest daughter of Joshua Holmes.
Died in this District, on the 21st of November, Mr. William E. Beamguard, son of Adam Beamguard, in the 21st year of his age.

Issue of December 11, 1856

Married on Tuesday, 9th instant, by Rev. W. W. Carothers, Rev. R. Y. Russell, of York District, to Miss Sarah N. Lewis, of Chester District.

Issue of December 18, 1856

Married in this District on the 9th ultimo, by John Roddy, Esq., Mr. Robert P. White,- and Miss Mary J. Cline.
Died in this District on the 1st instant, Mr. John D. Leech, third son of Joseph and Mary Leech, aged 18 years and 8 months.

Issue of December 25, 1856

Married on Thursday 18th instant, by Rev. Mr. Patterson, Capt. H. W. Campbell, of York and Miss Harriet Sims, of Lancaster.
On Thursday last,by the Rev. J. A. Hill, Mr. George Sturgis (Ebenezerville) and Mrs. E. Gaulden, all of this District.
On Thursday last, by John Roddy, Esq., Mr. J. C. McFadden and Miss Mary, daughter of A. T. Black, all of this District.

Issue of January 8, 1857

Married in this district on the 31st ult., by Rev. E. E. Boyce, Mr. James McElwee Sr., and Miss Nancy McElwee.
In this District on Sunday last,by Rev. J. R. Baird, Mr. Columbus Cook and Mrs. Mary A. Anderson, daughter of Samuel Burns Sen'r.
In Charleston, on Thursday the 25th ultimo, by the Rev. Dr. Bachman, Capt. Asbury Coward, of the King's Mountain Military School, and Miss Eliza Corbet, youngest daughter of Mr. John A. Blum.

41

On Tuesday, the 23d of December, by Rev. Donald McQueen, Rev.
James McDowell and Miss Mary Pauline, daughter of Dr. J. B.
Witherspoon, all of Sumter.
Died in this District on the 18th of December 1856, Mr.
William Patrick, in the 73d year of his age. During the war of
1812, Mr. Patrick was a Lieutenant in the Regiment of South
Carolina Militia in service at Charleston....
At Lancasterville, on Tuesday morning, the 30th ult., after
a lingering illness of one week, Mrs. Mary Elizabeth, wife of
James H. Witherspoon, Esq., Ordinary and Commissioner in Equity
for Lancaster District.

Issue of January 15, 1857

Married on the 18th of December, 1856, by Dr. Wilson, of
Georgia, Mr. S. A. McElwee and Miss S. A. Wilson, both of York
District.
Died at his residence in this District, on the 31st ult.,
William Bratton, in the 41st year of his age. The deceased has
left a wife and four small children...(eulogy)

Issue of January 22, 1857

Married in Columbia, on the evening of the 6th instant, by
the Very Rev. Dr. Lynch, Howard H. Caldwell, Esq., to Agnes,
second daughter of Charles Montague, Esq.
Married in Anderson District, on Wednesday evening last,by the
Rev. J. Scott Murray, J. V. Moore, Esq., (Editor of the True
Carolinian), to Miss E. E. Robinson, all of Anderson District.
The Starkville (Miss.) Advocate, contains the particulars of
the horrible murder of Robt. Burns, proprietor of the Cottage
Hotel in that place, by Dr. W. D. Stovall, with whom he had had
a fight the day before....(account).

Issue of January 29, 1857

Married in this District, on Thursday the 15th instant, by
Rev. S. L. Watson, Mr. John B. Alexander, of Cherokee County,
Alabama, and Miss Margaret Jane, youngest daughter of the late
Wm. Watson, of this district.
On the 8th instant, by Rev. F. A. McCorkle, Mr. William Ram-
say, of Columbia, S. C., to Miss Julia C., daughter of Dr. J. E.
Broyles of Greene county, Tenn.
Died in this District on the 22d instant, Mr. Joseph Boggs,
aged about 70 years.
In this District on the 21st instant, Mr. N. H. Horn, aged
about 40 years.
In this District on Saturday the 17th instant, Mrs. Mary H.
McNeel, wife of Mr. James G. McNeel, and daughter of Mr. John
McConnell, aged 29 years. Mrs. McNeel was a consistent member
of the Presbyterian Church....

Issue of February 5, 1857

Married on the 27th ultimo, by the Rev. John McLees, Mr. D.
Wyatt Aiken, of Winnsboro, and Miss V. C. Smith, daughter of the
late Joel Smith, Esq., of Stoney Point, Abbeville District, S. C.
Died of Typhoid Fever on the 31st ult., after an illness of
twenty-one days, at his residence in York District, James Moore,

Esq., in the seventy-second year of his age. The deceased was
a member of Bethesda Church for about fifty years, and a ruling
Elder in the same for more than forty....
     In this District on the 1st inst.,Mrs. Rebecca Robertson,
wife of the late Thomas Robertson, aged 75 years. She was a
member of the Baptist Church....

Issue of February 12, 1857

     Married in this District on the 5th instant, by Rev. S. L.
Watson, Mr. James A. Glenn, and Miss Nancy J. Mason, all of this
District.
     On the 5th instant, by Rev. R. F. Logan, Capt J. J. Strain,
of this District, to Miss M. S. J. Floyd, of Gaston Co., N. C.
     On the 5th ultimo, by Rev. R. P. Logan, Mr. J. L. Floyd, of
North Carolina, to Miss S. J., youngest daughter of James
Strain of this District.
     On the 29th ultimo, by Rev. R.Y. Russell, Mr. William T.
Thompson, to Miss Sallie J. Giles, all of Unionville.
     On the 4th inst., by Rev. William Martin, Capt. T. B. Jeter
to Miss Ann H. Thomson, all of Unionville.

Issue of February 19, 1857

     Married in Union County, North Carolina, on Tuesday the 10th
instant, by John Gordon, Esq., Capt. Julius Friedeman of "Mary,
Mine,"in this district, to Miss Elizabeth Wolf.
     On Wednesday evening, 11th inst., by the Rev. N. Talley,
Rev. John T. Wightman, of the South Carolina Methodist Conference,
to Miss Amelia, daughter of the Rev. H. Spain, of Sumter District,
S. C.
     On the 5th instant, by Rev. J. M. H. Adams, Mr. Edward R.
Mills, of Chester District, and Miss Mary Jane Moore, of York
District.
     Died in Yorkville, S. C., on the 13th instant, Mrs. Phoebe
DeWitt Moore, wife of Edward Moore, Esq., in the 20th year of her
age...a native of Society Hill, Darlington District, S. C...
(eulogy)
     Died in Chester, on the 11th inst., of Consumption, Mr. F.
M. Killian.
     At Bethel, in this District, on the 12th instant, of Pneumonia,
Mr. Jerome B. Brian, aged about 27 years.
     Died at his residence in this District on the 17th inst.,
Col. James M. Harris, in the 74th year of his age.

Issue of February 26, 1857

     Married on the 15th instant, by A. Hardin, Esq., Mr. Abraham
Skates, of Cleveland County, N. C. and Miss Elizabeth, daughter
of David and Elizabeth Skates, of this District.
     On Thursday the 19th instant, by Rev. S. C. Millen, Mr. S.
Neely Miller and Miss Eliza J., eldest daughter of James McElwee,
Sr., all of this District.

Issue of March 12, 1857

     Married on the 5th instant, by the Rev. S. L. Watson, Mr.
Leander W. Moore and Mis Drucilla E. Quinn, all of this District.
     On Tuesday 17th of February, by E. G. Brown, Esq., Mr. Wm.
Boyles, and Miss Jane Warlick, all of this District.

Died in this county, on the 26th ult., with Typhoid Pneumonia, produced by an attack of Measles, Wm. Ross Jr., youngest son of Wm. Ross, Esq., in the 29th year of his age, leaving an aged father and two brothers to mourn his loss. (eulogy). Mecklinburg, N. C., March 1, 1857.

Issue of March 19, 1857

Married on the 12th ultimo, by Rev. Arthur Small, Rev. D. Harrison, of Fairfield, and Miss Aurelia E. Patterson, of Liberty Hill, Kershaw District,S. C.
Died at Hoylesville, Gaston County, N. C., on the 19th ult., Andrew Hoyle, Esq., in the 87th year of his age...The Presbyterian Church in Dallas was built chiefly by himself....(long eulogy)
Charlotte Democrat.
Died in Bradley County, Arkansas, on the 24th of January, 1857, Sarah Ann Richardson, wife of Thomas A. Richardson, formerly of York Dist., So. Ca., aged 26 years, 10 months and 8 days....

Issue of March 26, 1857

Married in Philadelphia (Pa.), on the 4th of March inst., by Rev. Dr. Pope, Mr. Lewis Bloomberg, of Yorkville, S. C., and Miss Hanna, daughter of E. S. Solms, Esq., of the former place.

Issue of April 2, 1857

Married on Tuesday the 31st ult.,by the Rev. S. C. Millen, Mr. Stephen M. Johnston,to Miss Margaret, daughter of Mr. Richard M. Pressly, all of this district.
On Tuesday, the 31st ult., by Rev. S. L. Watson, Mr. William Moore and Miss Mary Patrick, all of this District.
Died in this District on Sunday the 22nd ultimo, Mr. Middleton McDaniel, aged about 57 years.

Issue of April 9, 1857

Died in Yorkville, on the 7th inst., after a short illness, Mr. Benjamin Franklin Withers, a native of the District, aged 30 years, 5 months and 11 days...left a young and devoted wife....

Issue of April 16, 1857

Died at Davidson College, N. C., April 5th, 1857, Morrison Hill, eldest child of Major D. H. and Isabella S. Hill, aged 6 years and 8 months....
Died in this District on Friday, 11th instant, Mr. Daniel P. Hall, in the 44th year of his age.
In DeSoto County, Mississippi, of Typhoid Fever, Miss Margaret Priscilla White, daughter of Moses and Sarah White, formerly of Lancaster District.

Issue of April 23, 1857

Married on Tuesday, 21st instant, by James Jefferys, Esq., Mr. James Harris and Miss Margaret Whitaker, all of this District.
In this district on the 15th instant, by Rev. R. Y. Russell, Dr. A. O. Walker of Union District, to Miss Mary A. Lowry, of Georgia.

Died in Pope County, Arkansas, on the morning of the 25th of
March ultimo, after a painful illness of thirteen days, Miss
Mary Clementine Fewel, in the 20th year of her age...born in York
District, S. C. (long eulogy).

Issue of April 30, 1857

Married on the 22d April, by Rev. M. D. Wood, of Walterborough,
S. C., Rev. John S. Harris and Miss Agnes, youngest daughter of
Mrs. H. Bratton, all of this District.
    At Mount Paran Church, on Friday the 17th of April, by Rev.
J. J. Jones, Mr. James Baber of North Caroline, and Miss Eugenia
Crow, of this District.
    Died in this District, on Friday, 24th instant, Mr. Sylvester
Hagans, aged about 55 years.
    At his residence in this District, suddenly, on the 21st
instant, Mr. James Craig, in the 85th year of his age.
    In Morganton, N. C., on Monday, 13th of April, of Bronchitis,
Edward Boone, only child of Joshua and Lucinda A. Stewart, aged
8 years and 1 month.

Issue of May 7, 1857

Married in Yorkville, on Tuesday morning, 5th instant, by Rev.
W. W. Carothers, Mr. Samuel W. Melton of the "Enquirer" and Miss
Mary Helen Goore, both of this place.
    On the evening of the 28th ultimo, by Rev. Jno. S. Harris, Mr.
William L. Sandifer, and Miss Lizzie A., daughter of Wm. Hanna,
Esq., all of this district.
    Also at the same time and place, and by the same minister,
Mr. J. Leonidas Moore, and Miss Ellen J. Hannah, all of this
District.
    Married at Lancasterville, on Wednesday evening of the 22nd
inst., by Rev. James H. Thornwell, D. D., John D. Wylie, Esq.,
and Miss Eliza Jane, daughter of James H. Witherspoon, Esq.
    On the 15th inst., by the Rev. David Wills, Capt. J. D. Gar-
lington, and Miss S. E. second daughter of Col. John D. Williams--
all of Laurens District.
    Died in this District on the evening of the 2d instant, after
a protracted illness, Mrs. Mary C. Adams, wife of Mr. S. Leroy
Adams, and daughter of the late Andrew Grier, Esq., of Mecklenburg
County, N. C., having just closed her 32d year...left a husband
and four small children....

Issue of May 14, 1857

Married on the 5th instant, at the house of John Porter, Sen.,
by Rev. W. C. Patterson, Mr. G. D. Brown, Esq., of Wolfville,
N. C., and Miss Mary P. Porter, of Lancaster, S. C.
    Died in this District on the 10th instant, Sarah Jane,
youngest daughter of Capt. James and Elizabeth Jackson, aged 11
months.
    On the 6th instant, at the residence of his father, in Colum-
bia, Thomas H., son of Samuel R. and M. A. Black, aged eight years.
    In Canton, Mississippi, at the residence of Hon. E. G. Henry,
on the 26th ult., Miss Nancy Henry, after a long and painful illness.

Issue of May 21, 1857

Married in Spartanburg on the 14th instant, Dr. Thomas B. Cureton, of Lancasterville and Miss Mary, only daughter of Major Govan Mills, of the former place.

In Chester District, on the 13th instant, by Rev. Jno. S. Harris, Mr. Samuel M. Hanna, of York District, and Miss Sallie A., youngest daughter of Mr. Alexander Pagan, of Chester District.

In Chester, on Monday evening, 18th instant, by Rev. Samuel Townsend, Mr. James Johnson, formerly of Charlotte, N. C., and Miss Mary, daughter of John D. Simril, of the former place.

Died in this District, on the 18th instant, Mrs. Mary Harshaw, aged 72 years, six months and twenty days...member of the Independent Presbyterian Church. (eulogy).

In Yorkville, on Tuesday morning, 19th instant, Mr. R. M. Walker, formerly of Cass Co., Ga., aged about 48 years.

Issue of May 28, 1857

Died on the 23d instant, at his residence in this District, Mr. Robert Adams, aged eighty seven years...(long eulogy).

Died at his residence in this District, on Saturday, 26th instant, George Wright, Esq., in the 84th year of his age.

Issue of June 4, 1857

Married on the 21st ultimo, by Rev. A. A. James, Mr. J. Madison Smarr, and Miss Martha Moss, all of this District.

Died in this District, on the 23d ultimo, Anrrew Hoyle, son of S. Leroy and Mary C. Adams, aged 3 months.

Issue of June 11, 1857

Married on Tuesday the 19th ult., by Rev. R. Y. Russell, Mr. S. B. Alexander and Miss Sallie A., youngest daughter of Reese Parker, Esq., all of Union District.

In Greensboro', N. C., on 21st May, Walter P. Caldwell, Attorney at Law, of Statesville and Miss Nannie E. Weatherly.

In the Chapel of Davidson College, N. C., by Rev. Dr. Lacy, Rev. S. C. Alexander, of Rowan, and Miss Mary Holmes Brown, of Fayetteville.

At the same time and place, by Rev. I. F. Rockwell, Mr. N. Allison Clark, of Plainville, Conn., and Miss Hattie S. Rockwell, niece of the officiating minister.

On Thursday the 4th instant, by James Jefferys, Esq., Mr. John B. Wylie, and Miss Rebecca Jane Strait, all of this District.

Died in Mecklenburg, N. C., near Davidson College, Mrs. Elizabeth Gillespie, wife of Joseph Gillespie, Esq., about 30 years of age.

Issue of June 18, 1857

Married in Clinton County, Illinois, on the 21st of May, by Rev. J. Hassenger, of Delaware, Mr. D. F. Davis, and Miss Elizabeth R. Clark, both formerly of York District, S. C.

Died on Sunday, the 15th inst., at the residence of her son, John Barron, Mrs. Fanny Barron, in the 80th year of her age. For the past three years she has resided with her son, Dr. Barron, of our village...(eulogy)

Issue of June 25, 1857

Died on Wednesday morning, 17th instant, at 3 o'clock, at the residence of his daughter, Mrs. Elizabeth E. Gillespie, Mr. Major T. Hall, in the 76th year of his age...member in the Presbyterian Church for several years. He left 5 children and many near relatives....

Issue of July 2, 1857

Married in Chester, S. C., on the 16th ultimo, by Rev. J. D. Gibson, Mr. Thos. DeGraffenreid, of Chester, S. C., and Miss Belvidera J., daughter of Col. Wm. Gott, formerly of Greensborough.

On Tuesday morning, the 2nd of June, by Rev. J. M. Young, Rev. H. Quigg, Pastor of Hopewell church, Newton County, Ga., and Miss S. A., daughter of R. G. Craig, Esq., of Dallas County, Alabama.

On the 25th of June by Rev. W. C. Patterson, Robt. M. Sims and Miss Kate C. Lucky, all of Lancaster district, S. C.

Died in this place on Friday morning, 25th ultimo, Mrs. Margaret C. Lester, wife of Rev. A. H. Lester, of the South Carolina Conference, aged 22 years, 11 months and 4 days....

Issue of July 9, 1857

Died in Portsmouth,Va., on the first of June, John R. Traylor, second son of W. B. And Lucinda Traylor, aged 24 years. The deceased was raised in York District, but for the last ten months has been employed on the Portsmouth and Weldon Railroad....

Issue of July 16, 1857

Died in Chester, on Tuesday, 14th inst., Mrs. Emeline Lowe, wife of G. W. Lowe.

Issue of July 23, 1857

Married on the morning of the 21st instant, by Rev. John S. Harris, Mr. Jno. L. Starr, and Miss Mary F. Sandifer, all of this District.

Died in Gaston Co., N. C., on the 11th inst., Charles Sandifer, son of R. G. and O. E. McLean, aged 18 months and 11 days.

At Aiken, on the 18th inst., Harriet Behethland Hagood, only child of Johnson, and Eloise B. Hagood, aged 1 years and 1 month.

Issue of July 30, 1857

Married on the 21st instant, by Rev. Albert A. James, A. Haywood Gaither, Esqr. of Morganton, N. C., and Miss Corrie Hoey, of Union District, S. C.

Died in Abbeville District, on June 23d, 1857, Mary Elizabeth Clinckscales, second daughter of G. B. Clinckscales, Esq., aged twenty years one month and seven days.

Issue of August 6, 1857

Married on the 22d ult., by the Rev. Toliver Robinson, Dr. J. S. Wolff, and Miss Bettie, eldest daughter of Col. J. and Mrs. C. H. Hudgens, all of Laurens.

Died in Rusk county, Texas, on the 4th of June last, of Dropsy, Miss Margaret E. Lacy, formerly of York District.

Issue of August 13, 1857

Married on Wednesday, 5th instant, by Jas. Jefferys, Esq., Mr. Chesterfield Lanier, and Miss Amanda Woods, all of this District.

Died in this place on Wednesday morning, 12th instant, Mrs. Sarah Hare, aged about 68 years.

Issue of August 20, 1857

Married in Union District, on the 6th inst., by Rev. R. A. Ross, Major T. P. Whitesides, of York, and Miss M. E. Patrick, of the former District.

Died in Yorkville, on Thursday, 18th instant, Mary, eldest daughter of Mr. M. & M. J. Jones, aged 3 years, and 4 months.

In this place on the 12th instant, George Pressley, youngest son of Dr. A. I. and Mary Barron, aged 8 months.

Near Bethel, in this District, on Monday morning, 17th instant, Mrs. Jane Glenn, wife of Henry Glenn, aged about 40 years.

In this District on Monday, 17th instant, Margaret Amarintha, second daughter of Maj. John B. and Amarintha Lowry, aged 8 years.

Issue of August 27, 1857

Married on Tuesday evening, 11th instant, at the residence of the bride's father, by Rv. L. C. Hinton, Mr. S. W. Mobley, of Chester, and Miss M. E., daughter of Capt. C. J. Kee, of York District.

On the 20th instant, by Rev. E. E. Boyce, Mr. Robert Pursley, and Miss Jane Lessley, all of this District.

Died on Tuesday, 18th instant, Mrs. Sarah Harper, wife of R. J. Harper, aged about 37 years.

In this District on the 18th instant, Mrs. Salena Ford, in the 46th year of her age.

In this District on the 20th instant, John Hill, only son of John C. and Frances McCarter, aged 11 months.

Issue of September 3, 1857

Married on Friday 28th ult., by James Jefferys, Esq., Mr. Nathaniel Smith and Mrs. Elizabeth C. Reynolds, all of this District.

Died in Lincoln County, North Carolina, Mrs. Catharine A. McLean, wife of Dr. William B. McLean, on the morning of the 18th August 1857....Catharine Allison Hope was born October 31, 1812, in Chester District, South Carolina. In very early life, she connected herself with the church of Bethesda. She was married December 29th, 1835, to James M. Stringfellow. Two lovely children, the fruit of this marriage, died in infancy, and left her childless.... Mr. Stringfellow died 24th of November 1844... married to Dr. Mc. B. McLean, of Lincoln County, N. C., on 3 February 1848...stepmother to six children....(long account and eulogy).

Died of Dysentary, in Lancaster District, on the 6th instant, John Robert, infant son of R. H. Porter.

In this district, on the 27th instant, an infant daughter of James Janes, aged five weeks.

Issue of September 10, 1857

Died in Charlotte, N. C., on the 28th ultimo, of Consumption, Mr. James Brian, aged 35 years.

Near Monk's Hill, in this District, on the 7th instant, Mrs. Margaret Whitesides, aged about 50 years.

On the 8th instant, near Antioch, in this District, Mr. Madison Hambright, of flux.

Issue of September 17, 1857

Married on Thursday evening, the 18th September, by the Rev. R. W. Brice, J. L. Gaston, Esq., of Chester, to Miss Margaret B. Hemphill, of Fairfield, S. C.

Died in Yorkville, on Saturday morning, 12th instant, Anna Bryon, youngest daughter of Mr. C. B. and Mrs. A. B. Knowles, aged about 14 months.

In this District on the 15th instant, at the residence of Mr. Richard Sadler, Franklin Davidson, infant son of Dr. A. C. and Margaret R. McRee.

Issue of September 24, 1857

Died in Chester, on Sabbath afternoon, the 18th instant, of Typhoid Diarrhoe, Mrs. Sarah Ann, late wife of R. W. Murray, and daughter of Wm. Farrar, deceased, in the 23d year of her age...a member of the Methodist Church...two children of hers, who passed from earth about one year ago.

In this District, on the 18th inst., Mrs. Frances C. Love, wife of Dr. R. L. Love, and daughter of John and Jane Smarr, aged 21 years, 4 months and 12 days.

Issue of October 1, 1857

Married on Thursday, the 24th ultimo, at the residence of the father of the bride, by James Jefferys, Esq., Mr. James Garvin, and Miss Elizabeth C. Miskelly, all of this District.

On the same day, at the same place, by James Jefferys, Esq., Mr. John W. Miskelly, and Miss Adeline Wood, all of this District.

Died at his residence in this village, on Tuesday, the 22nd inst., Col. William Wright, in the 59th year of his age...born in York District about 13 miles north west of the Court House, but his father and family removing to the village in his early infancy, he afterwards lived and died a citizen of Yorkville... (long account and eulogy).

Near Crowder's Creek, on the 12th ultimo, Mr. Ellis Howel, aged 50 years.

Issue of October 8, 1857

Married at Fort Mill, on Thursday, 24th ultimo, by E. J. Patterson, Esq., Mr. David H. McCree and Mrs. Margaret M. Carrigan, both of Mecklenburg, N. C.

Died, after a very short illness, while on a visit in Yorkville, on the evening of the 31st ultimo, Mrs. Elvira, wife of Joseph C. Johnson, Esq., aged about 43 years.

In this District, near Blairsville, on the 4th instant, at the residence of her son, R. A. Lathem, Mrs. Sarah Lathem, aged 66 years.

In this District, on the 2d instant, of abdominal dropsy,

Mrs. Susan Williams, in the 45th year of her age.

Issue of October 15, 1857

Death of Dr. L. F. Barnett...on Sunday night last. He was a native of Spartanburg,but adopted Yorkville as his home....

Married at Fort Mill on Tuesday, 6th instant, by Joseph F. White, Esq., Mr. Julius Griffin, and Miss Purnet Wyatt, both of "Kansas."

Died on the 5th inst., in the 46th year of her age, Mrs. Nancy Hannah, wife of Rev. S. L. Watson, Pastor of Bethel Church, in this District. (eulogy)

In this District on the 6th instant, George, infant son of B. F. and L. E. Rawlinson, aged 11 months and 20 days.

Issue of October 29, 1857

Married on the 22d instant, by Rev. J. D. Hall, Mr. J. W. Ferell of York District, S. C., and Miss Jane J. Smith of Gaston Co., N. C.

At the residence of the bride's father, in this District, on the 27th instant, by Rev. John S. Harris, Capt. Wm. H. Poag, and Miss Mary R., daughter of Capt. I. N. Sadler, all of this District.

On the 28th instant, by Rev. R. F. Taylor, Col. Alexander Ramsay, of Kent county, Tennessee, and Miss Nannie R., youngest daughter of Richard M. Pressley, Esq. of York Dist.

Died of typhoid fever, at the residence of Mrs. Polly Burris, in this District, on the 14th inst., Mrs. Mary M. Burris...member of the Independent Presbyterian Church...Her father Mr. Edward Burris, far advanced in life, still survives. Her mother, Mrs. Elizabeth Burris has for yeasr forgotten the tears of sorrow, in the joyrs of Heaven.

Issue of November 5, 1857

Married near Ebenezerville, on the 28th ultimo, by Rev. J. G. Richards, Mr. S. M. Mills and Miss Mary I. Harris (Bell) all of York District.

On the 20th ultimo, by Rev. Dr. Kerr, Mr. Robert Davis, of Gaston Co., N. C., and Miss Pamela Thomas, of this District.

Died in Union District, on Sunday morning 25th ultimo, Nancy Harriet, infant daughter of Mrs. Lizzie and Col. J. Felix Walker.

On the 27th ultimo, near Horn Lake, DeSoto County,Miss., Mr. Stephen McCorkle, in the 65th year of his age.

Issue of November 12, 1857

Died on Pneumonia, at the residence of her husband, Mr. M. Elder, in this village, on Friday afternoon the 6th instant, Mrs. Jane Elder, aged 37 years...member of the Associate Reformed Church....

Died on Monday evening, Nov. 2d, James L., infant son (the last only only remaining child) of Mrs. Lizzie and J. Felix Walker, of this District.--Unionville Journal.

Issue of November 19, 1857

Married on the 12th instant, by Rev. W. W. Carothers, Mr.
M. L. Tate, and Miss Nancy Thomasson, all of this district.

Issue of November 26, 1857

Married in Benton County, Ala., on the 25th of September,
by Rev. N. A. Davis, Mr. Robert M. Hanna, and Miss Mary E. Smith,
all of that county.
On the same day, by the same person, in the same county, Mr.
James J. Henderson and Miss Mary Elizabeth Hanna.
Died in Paris, Texas, on the 29th ult., Mrs. Mary Jane, wife
of Hon. John T. Mills.

Issue of December 3, 1857

Married on the 25th of November, by the Rev. Mr. McCormick, Mr.
James L. Barry, of Arkansas (formerly of York), to Miss Sue
Carlisle, of Chester.
In this place on Thursday, 26th ultimo, by James Jefferys,
Esq., Mr. Ebenezer Adams, and Miss Mary C. Henderson, all of
Yorkville.
In Fairfield, on Tuesday, 24th ultimo, by Rev. J. R. Castles,
Mr. J. M. Whitesides of York, and Miss Margaret Castles, of the
former place.
In this district, on Tuesday 24th ultimo, by Ezekiel Fewell,
Esq., Mr. James Warren, and Miss Harriet Matthews, all of this
district.
In Columbia, on the afternoon of the 1st inst., by the Rev.
Dr. Thornwell, Col. W. W. Garvin, of Barnwell and Mrs. Kate
Ratchford, of Yorkville.

Issue of December 10, 1857

Married on Tuesday, 1st instant, by Rev. J. D. Hall, Mr.
John L. Watson, of York District, S. C., and Miss Mollie M., only
daughter of Mr. Andrew Neagle of Gaston county, N. C.
In Charleston, on Thursday evening, 3d instant, by Rev. U.
Sinclair Bird, Wm. B. Carlise, Esq., Assistant editor of the
Courier, and Arabella, third daughter of Wm. Bird, Esq.,all of
that city.
On the 3d instant, by James Jefferys, Esq., Mr. William H.
Wilson, and Miss Rhoda E. Parrott, all of this District.
On the 6th instant, by James Jefferys, Esq., Mr. David Pierson,
of Shelby county, Alabama, and Miss Elizabeth H. Habsheer, of this
District.
In this District, on Tuesday evening, 8th inst., by Rev.
Joseph Holmes, Mr. Thomas Dickson, and Miss Mary E. Howell, all
of this District.

Issue of December 17, 1857

Married on the 8th instant, by Rev. W. W. Carothers, Mr.
Samuel C. Youngblood, of Mecklenburg county, N. C., and Miss Mary
O. Choat, of this District.
On Thursday, 10th inst., by Rev. E. E. Boyce, Mr. S. Wilson
Love and Miss Margaret A. Torrence, all of Gaston County, N. C.
Died in this District on the 6th inst., Mrs. Rachael Barnett,
in the 81st year of her age.

Issue of December 24, 1857

Married on the 22d instant, by Rev. James A. Davies, Mr. J. W. Beamguard, and Miss D. C. Stevenson, all of this District.

Issue of January 7, 1858

Married in Union District, on Wednesday evening, 16th ultimo, by Rev. W. W. Carothers, Mr. Samuel E. Goudelock, and Miss N. Jane Parker.

On the 8th ultimo, by Rev. G. K. Andrews, Mr. Robert M. Finley, of Marion, N. C., and Miss Sarah A. Melton, of Rutherford, N. C.

Died in DeSoto County, Miss., on the 26th ultimo, Mrs. A. J. Miller, consort of Dr. Joseph D. Miller, formerly of this district.

In this District on the 6th inst., Edward Dewit, infant son of Edward Moore, Esqr.

Issue of January 14, 1858

Married on the 7th instant, by Wm. McGill, Esq., Mr. Robert A. Millen, of Gaston, N. C., and Miss Margaret Hays, of York Dist.

Died in this District on Sunday, 10th instant, Mr. John Phifer (Shoe-maker) aged about 60 years.

David C. Carson, departed this life on the 5th of January, 1858. He was born October 16th, 1777. He went to Charleston as a voluntter during the war of 1812.

Issue of January 21, 1858

Married on Tuesday, 12th instant, by Rev. S. L. Watson, Mr. A. W. Matthews and Miss Henrietta C. Hudson, all of this District.

On Thursday 14th by Rev. S. L. Watson, Mr. Jno. Dulin, and Miss Mary J. McCullough, all of this district.

Issue of January 28, 1858

Married on Thursday, 22d instant, by J. D. P. Currence, Esq., Mr. Wm. A. Brandon and Miss Polly Wallace, all of this District.

Died on the first day of January last, at her residence in Canton, Miss., in the 69th year of her age, Mrs. Harriet Chambers, wife of Benjamin Chambers, Esq., formerly of Yorkville, S. C. (long eulogy)

Issue of February 4, 1858

Married on the 26th ult., by the Rev. John S. Harris, Mr. James Erwin, and Miss Jane Hemphill, all of this District.

In Chester District, on the 26th ultimo, by Rev. Mr. Bell, Mr. George W. Melton, of Yorkville, and Miss Fannie Poag of Chester District.

On the evening of the 2nd instant, by Reverend John S. Harris, Mr. Nathaniel Johnston, of Cabarrus Co., N. C., and Miss Mary E., eldest daughter of Joseph C. Johnston, Esq., of York District, S. C.

Died in Yorkville on the 29th ultimo, Ida C., infant daughter of William A. and Nancy C. Wright, aged 2 years and 7 months.

Issue of February 11, 1858

Married on the 4th instant, by Thos. McGill, Esq., Mr. James Fayssoux, and Miss Jemima, second daughter of Morgan and Polly Dover, all of this District.

In Chester District on the 2d instant, by Rev. J. S. Bailey, Mr. W. Holmes Hardin, and Miss Martha Guy, all of that district.

In Lancaster, on the 14th of January, at the residence of Rev. Adam Ivey, by Rev. William C. Patterson, Dr. J. N. Nesbitt, and Miss Mary Jane Phifer.

At Liberty Hill, Kershaw District, S. C., by Rev. Arthur Small, Col. Robert B. Dunningham, and Miss Mary Small, of Charleston.

In this District on Tuesday 9th instant, by Rev. O. A. Darby, Mr. David J. Logan, of Cleveland Co., N. C., and Miss Sallie, daughter of B. D. Rowell, Es q. of York District.

Died in Columbia, S. C., on the 26th of January, of consumption, Samuel E. Stratton, proprietor of the Washington House, aged 43 years. He was a antive of Bridgeport, Connecticut, but for the last 25 years an esteemed resident of Columbia....(eulogy).

Issue of February 18, 1858

Married on the 16th instant, by Rev. Jno. S.Harris, Mr. D. A. Gordon, of Yorkville, to Mrs. Sallie E. McNeel, daughter of Jno. McConnell, Esq., of this District.

On the evening of the same day, by the same, at the house of Robt. M. Lindsay, Esq., of this District, Mr. Edward Crawford, of Chester District, and Miss Henrietta E. Lindsay, of this District.

Issue of February 25, 1858

Married on the 4th inst., Mr. W. W. McEleee and Miss Mollie Jane Wilson, all of this District.

Died on the 12th instant, at Ebenezer, in this District, William Smith, youngest child of Rev. John G. and Mrs. Sophia E. Richards, aged thirteen months and thirteen days....

Issue of March 4, 1858

Married on the 23d ultimo, at the residence of Joel S. Barnett, Esq., by Rev. J. G. Richards, Mr. Reece W. Workman, and Miss Martha A. Barnett, all of this District.

In this District on the 25th ultimo, by Rev. J. G. Richards, Mr. Hilary Kirkpatrick, and Miss Cyntha Agers, all of this District.

Died in this District on the 27th ultimo, Susan R., daughter of Wm. A. and P. E. Workman, aged two years, six months and six days.

Issue of March 11, 1858

Married in Union District on the 4th inst.,by Rev. O. A. Darby, Mr. B. Derrer of Yorkville, to Miss Sarintha N. Howell, of the former district.

In this District on the 23d ultimo, by Rev. S. L. Watson, Mr. R. L. Simmons, and Mrs. M. C. Brian, all of this District.

Died near Tulip, Dallas County, Ark., on the 12th February, 1858, John Harris, son of Joseph and Margaret M. Doby, in the sixth year of his age....

Issue of March 18, 1858

Married on Thursday evening, 11th instant, by Rev. J. M. H. Adams, Mr. J. M. Henderson, of Mecklenburg Co., N. C., and Miss Leonora E. Simril, of Yorkville.

Married in Yorkville, on the 23d ult., by Rev. J. M. H. Adams, Rev. William B. Corbett and Miss Lizzie, daughter of Col. I. D. Witherspoon.

Issue of March 25, 1858

Married on Tuesday, 16th instant, by Rev. J. J. Jones, Mr. Summy Russ, of Cleveland Co., N. C., and Miss Elizabeth Carroll, of York District, S. C.

On Tuesday 22d instant, Mr. Robert A. Black, and Miss Martha daughter of Wm. Berry, Esq., all of this district.

Mrs. Elizabeth Love, died in Yorkville, S. C., 18th March in the 31st year of her age. A husband, brothers and friends mourn her....

Issue of April 1, 1858

Married on Wednesday morning last, 24th ultimo, about 1 o' clock a. m., by S. L. Love, Esq., Mr. Edward Owens, and Miss Margaret Warlick, all of this district.

In Charlotte, N. C., on the 25th ultimo, by Rev. Mr. Griffith, Mr. John T. Harry, and Miss Susan E. Shelby, of Tennessee.

Issue of April 8, 1858

Married on Thursday, 1st instant, by Rev. J. R. Castles, Mr. J. T. Whitesides, and Miss Sallie Crosby, all of this District.

On the 30th ultimo, by Wm. McGill, Esq., Mr. Wm. F. Millen, of Gaston Co., N. C., and Miss Elizabeth Clark, of York District.

On Tuesday, the 12th of January last, by Rev. H. Walsh, Dr. Fayette Gabbert, of Arkansas, and Miss Mary Jane, daughter of the late Dr. Stephen McCorkle, of DeSoto county, Miss.

On Wednesday morning, 10th ultimo, at the residence of the bride's father, by Rev. H. Walsh, Mr. Jos. M. McCorkle, and Miss Jennie, daughter of A. R. Hutchinson, all of DeSoto Co., Miss.

On Wednesday morning, 10th ultimo, at the residence of the bride's father, by Rev. H. Walsh, Mr. Wesley A. Winberly, of Ashley Co., Arkansas and Miss Mollie M. Hutchinson, youngest daughter of A. R. Hutchinson, of DeSoto county, Mississippi.

Issue of April 15, 1858

Died in Yorkville on Friday 9th instant, after a short illness, Mr. James McLure, aged about 45 years.

Issue of April 22, 1858

Married on Tuesday 20th instant, by Rev. J. A. Davies, Dr. Lawson A. Hill, and Miss Barbara Whisonant, all of this District.

Died after a short illness, Mrs. Jane Eliza Neely, wife of Thomas McLure, Jr. She was born May 1st, 1835, and died March 16th, 1858, aged 23 years, 10 months and 16 days. (long eulogy)

Died in this District on the 9th inst., Capt. Robert Caldwell, in the 72d year of his age...Presbyterian Church. (eulogy).

Died in Athens, Geo., of scarlet fever, on Thursday, April

the 6th 1858, John Thomas Jefferson, infant son of Wm. S. and
Sarah A. Hemphill, aged 1 year, 7 months and 12 days.

Issue of April 29, 1858

Married on Thursday 22d instant, by Rev. J. A. Davies, Mr
Wm. B. Davidson, and Miss Sallie S., second daughter of the late
Hugh Allison, deceased, all of this District.
In this vicinity of Charlotte, N. C., on the 15th instant, by
Rev. J. Monroe Anderson, James M. Hutchison, Esq.,and Miss Lizzie
J., daughter of Maj. Benj. Morrow.
On the 15th instant, by Rev. R. J. Meynardie, Thomas McCully,
Esq., of Chesterville, and Miss Sallie A. M.,daughter of Adam T.
Walker, Esq., of Chester District, S. C.
Died in this District, on Thursday 15th inst., after an ill-
ness of 45 days, Mrs. Jane Finley, wife of James Finely, aged
about 43 years.

Issue of May 6, 1858

Married on Thursday evening 29th ultimo, by Rev. J. J. Jones,
Mr. H. K. McSwain, of Cleveland Co., N. C., ad Miss Catharine
Davies, of York District.
On the 28th ultimo, by James Jefferys, Esq., Mr. Wylie
Whyatt, and Miss Martha Wilson, all of this District.

Issue of May 13, 1858

Married on Thursday, 6th instnat, by Rev. E. E. Boyce, Capt.
W. T. Davis, and Miss M. J. Wilson, of Caston county, N. C.
In Chester, on Sunday, 2d instant, by Wm. H. Anderson, Esq.,
Mr. George W. Lowe, and Miss Margaret, daughter of J. A. Estes,
Esq.

Issue of May 27, 1858

Married on Thursday 20th instant, by Wm. McGill, Esq., Mr.
J. P. Horton, and Miss Mary D. Fairess, all of this district.
On Tuesday, 18th instant, by Rev. R. A. Ross, Mr. Samuel
Larthrage, and Miss Nancy Scott, all of this District.
Near Ebenezerville, on Tuesday, 18th instant, by Rev. J. G.
Richards, Mr. Daniel C. Williams of Yorkville and Miss Mary J.,
daughter of the late Wm. S. May, of the former place.
Died in Yorkville, on Saturday, 15th instant, Mrs. Margaret
S., wife of the late Robert Morrow, aged 62 years.
In this place on Friday, 14th instant, William Dickson,
youngest child of W. D. and Mary J. Miller, aged about 15 months.
In this District on Sunday, 23d instant, Margaret G., daughter
of Wm. A. H. and M. J. Wilson, aged 1 year and 15 days.

Issue of June 3, 1858

Married on the 6th ultimo, by Rev. B. Bonner, Mr. Joseph H.
Austell, of Spartanburg District, and Miss Mary Jane Borders, of
Cleveland County, N. C.

Issue of June 10, 1858

Died in this District on the 3d instant, Mr. John Hambright,
aged 72 years.

Issue of June 17, 1858

Married on Tuesday 8th instant, by John R. Wallace, Mr. J. J. Parrot, and Miss Nancy A. Monroe, all of this district.

On Thursday evening, 10th instant, by James Jefferys, Esq., Mr. Marcus Derrer, and Miss Sarintha N. Derrer, all of this District.

Died at the residence of her mother, in Iredell Co., N. C., May 20th, 1858, Mrs. Susan McNinch, wife of James McNinch (formerly Miss Susan Quinn), in the 20th year of her age.

Issue of June 24, 1858

Died on Saturday morning, 19th instant, a son of Robert M. and Mary Wilson, aged about one year.

Issue of July 1, 1858

Married on Tuesday, 22d ultimo, by Rev. S. L. Watson, Mr. W. Independence Stowe, of Gaston, N. C. and Miss I. Caroline Hunter of Bethel, S. C.

Died in York District, Mrs. Mary Palmer Sandifer, consort of Green Sandifer, in the 67th year of her age....

In this district on Sunday 27th ultimo, James Bolivar, son of Mrs. J. B. Eddins, aged 4 months and 22 days.

Issue of July 8, 1858

Married on the morning of the 24th ultimo, in the Baptist Church, by the Rev. Dr. Curtis, Mr. John McKee Jr.,and Miss Eugenia Hinton, all of Chester.

On the 27th of May, by Geo. L. McNeel, Esq., Mr. Washington Owens, and Miss Hannah Swett, daughter of Moses Swett, all of Chester District.

Issue of July 14, 1858

Died in Yorkville, on Tuesday morning, 6th inst., William Hugh, second child of W. K. and Charlotte J. Hackett, aged 6 months and 22 days.

At Glenn Springs, on the 8th instant, of Chronic Diarrhoe, Dr. Wm. Lowndes Black, in the 33d year of his age.

Issue of July 22, 1858

Married on Tuesday 20th instant, by Rev. James A. Davies, Mr. Lawson Clark and Miss Amanda Stevenson, all of this District.

Issue of August 12, 1858

Married on Thursday, 1st ultimo, by Rev. A. Enloe, at the house of the bride's father, Dr. Joseph D. Miller (formerly of York District, S. C.) to Miss Lucie Ann Stevens, all of DeSoto County, Mississippi.

Died at Rock Hill, on the 27th ultimo, Ida Amelia, infant daughter of H. F. and Mrs. Amelia L. Broach, aged 9 months and 22 days....

In Gaston County, North Carolina, on Saturday, 7th instant, Mr. D. Porter Morrow, aged about 40 years.

In Charleston,on the 3d instant, Frank Eugene, youngest son

of James M. A. and Eugenia Henderson, aged 7 months.

Issue of August 19, 1858

Married on Tuesday, 10th instant, by Rev. R. Y. Russell, Mr.
J. A. Lockhart, and Miss Nancy Thomas, all of this District.
In this District on the 22nd ultimo, by William McGill, Esq.,
Mr. Jonathan J. Hays, and Miss Nancy Cobb, both of Cleveland,
N. C.
On the 12th instant, by William McGill, Esq., Mr. John E.
Cook, and Miss Elizabeth E. Foy, both of Gaston, N. C.

Issue of August 26, 1858

Married on the 19th instant, by Rev. S. L. Watson, Mr. J. J.
Howe, and Miss Arraminta M. Quinn, all of this district.
In Union District, on the 10th instant, by Rev. R. W. Thompson,
Mr. Eli W. Fullenwider of Shelby, N. C., and Mrs. Mary C. McConnell,
of Union, S. C.
Died in this district, on the 15th of July last, Mr. Rufus
Cain, aged about 80 years.
In this district, on Sunday, 15th instant, Mr. Valentine Ful-
ler, aged 55 years.
In this District on the 15th of July, Nancy K., daughter of
Samuel K. and Elizabeth Gill, aged 6 years.
In this district, on the 22d instant, Mr. John Alexander,
aged about 55 years.
In this Distirct on the 23d instant, Mrs. Rachel Milliner, aged
about 57 years.

Issue of September 2, 1858

Married in Chester, on Tuesday, 26th ultimo, by Rev. L. C.
Hinton, Capt. W. H. Gill and Miss Margaret, daughter of the late
Maj. W. D. Henry.
On the 17th ultimo, by Rev. L. C. Hinton, Mr. Turner Barber
of Chester District, and Miss P. E. Kee, daughter of Capt. C. J.
Kee, of York.
Died in Yorkville, on Wednesday evening, 25th of August, Miss
Amanda A., daughter of the late Daniel and Holly B. Murphy, aged
twenty years and nine months....

Issue of September 9, 1858

Died in this District on the 2nd instant, Mrs. M. E. Bigger,
wife of A. B. Bigger, aged 33 years.

Issue of September 16, 1858

Married on Tuesday, 7th instant, at Capt. J. W. A. Hariness',
by Sam'l. G. Brown, Esq., Mr. S. A. McLuney, and Miss S. A.
Coln, all of this District.
Died Suddenly, near Hopewell, in this District, on Sunday
last, Dr. Samuel Wright, in the 55th year of his age.
In this District on the 14th instant, Charles Isaiah, son of
Dr. C. L. Clawson, aged fifteen months.

Issue of September 23, 1858

Married on Tuesday 14th instant, by Hugh Simpson, Esq., Mr. James W. Collins, and Miss Elizabeth Cathcart, all of this District.

On the 20th instant, by S. G. Brown, Esq., Mr. Wm. M. Dover, and Miss Nancy J. Hartness, all of this District.

In this District, on the 14th instant, by Rev. S. L. Watson, Thomas H. Grier, Esq., of Mecklenburg county, N. C., to Miss M. Catharine Barnett, of York District.

Died in this District on the 19th inst., William Wright, only child of Mr. S. A. and S. A. McElwee, aged 11 months and 11 days.

Suddenly, in this District, on the 20th instant, Mrs. Dorcas Smith, in her 76th year.

Issue of September 30, 1858

Married in Yorkville, S. C., on Tuesday evening, 28th instant, by Rev. R. A. Ross, John G. Enloe, Esq., and Miss Mary Ann, eldest daughter of the late Wm. R. Alexander, Esq., all of this place.

On the 23d instant, by Rev. J. A. Davies, Mr. Terrel Camp, of Cleveland county, N. C., and Miss Eliza C. Turner, of this District.

Died on Friday night last, at the residence of his grandfather, James Brian, Esq., Monroe Butler, son of James T. and Elizabeth Brian, aged about 11 years.

In Madison county, Mississippi, on the 15th instant, Mrs. Elizabeth Dinkins, consort of Mr. Lewis Dinkins.

Issue of October 14, 1858

Married in Yorkville, on Thursday last,7th instant, by Rev. J. M. H. Adams, Mr. E. Peyton Moore and Miss Lizzie Neely, all of this place.

Died on the 12th of September, in York District, S. C., Dr. Samuel Wright, in the 55th year of his age...member of the Presbyterian Church. The last time he was permitted to attend the sanctuary he dedicated his little daughter Perla to the service of God in baptism....

In Chester District of Quincy, on the 27th ult., William Alexander, son of Samuel J. and Mary J. Hemphill, formerly of York District, aged 3 years, five months and twelve days.

In Shelby county, Alabama, on the 1st instant, of congestive fever, Mr. Robert McLelland, formerly of York District.

In this District, on the 24th ult., Mrs. Mary McWhorter, aged 98 years.

Issue of October 28, 1858

Married on the afternoon of the 20th instant, at the house of Mr. H. I. Swann, by Rev. John S. Harris, Mr. Robert L. Davidson, and Miss Mary R. Latimer, all of this district.

On the 21st instant, by J. P. Hood, Esq., Mr. Leander Jones and Miss Elizabeth, eldest daughter of James and Martha Archer, all of this District.

Died at her residence in Lowndes Co., Mississippi, on the 2d instant, Abigail M., youngest daughter of Rev. William C. Davis, and consort of Rev. S. J. Feemster, aged 52 years, eleven months and four days.

Issue of November 4, 1858

Married on the 26th October by Rev. P. H. Pickett, at his residence in Chester District, Rev. A. H. Lester, of the South Carolina Conference, and Miss Sue McCullough, of Williamsburg District.

Died in Tippah County, Miss., on the 18th ultimo, John Franklin, only child of J. H. & A. L.Hill, aged 2 years, 3 months and one day.

October 5th, at the residence of Wm. G. Beckwith, Esq., Prattville, Ala.,Professor Josiah Harris, in the 63d year of his age. He was a native of York District, a graduate of Hamden Sidney College and of the Theological Seminary of Virginia.

Issue of November 11, 1858

Married at the residence of Dr. J. W. Tracy, in Cleveland County, N. C., on the 2d instant, by Rev. James D. Hall, Dr. J. L. Neagle of Gaston county, N. C., and Miss M. Love Stowe, of Cedar Springs, Spartanburg District, S. C.

In Columbia, on the 3d instant, by Rev. J. M. Pringle, Dr. J. B. Jennings of Bennettsville, to Miss Sallie A. McCully, of the former place.

Departed this life on the 21st of September, in Madison County, Miss., Laban Suggs, son of Capt. John and Martha J. Miller, aged 3 years, 6 months and 27 days.

In this District on the 8th instant, Mr. Joseph Black, aged about 55 years.

Issue of November 18, 1858

Married in Cleveland county, North Carolina, on the 11th instant, by Rev. A. A. McSwain, Mr. I. N. Hopper, and Miss Permelia J., daughter of Montgomery Starnes.

On the 11th instant, by Rev. A. A. McSwain, Mr. Samuel O. McSwain, and Miss Nancy Ann, daughter of Joab Hopper, all of Cleveland County, N. C.

On the 4th instant, by Rev. Landy Wood, Mr. Sylvester Caten, and Miss Louisa Jane, daughter of Mr. Joseph Thomas, all of this district.

Died in this District on the 11th instant, Nannah Little, daughter of Mr. Joseph W. and Mrs. Margaret W. Steele,aged eleven months....

Died in York District, on the 3d instant, of croup, Swanson Lunsford, son of Dr. J. C. and Mrs. R. Hicklin, aged 2 years and three months....

Issue of November 25, 1858

Wednesday morning last, Mr. James Strain, a citizen of the Indian Land, committed suicide...about 55 years of age...leaves a wife and large family.

Married in Yorkville on the 23d instant, by Rev. Jno. W. Kelly, Rev. O. A. Darby of the South Carolina Conference, and Mrs. R. Catharine Withers, of this place.

On Thursday evening, 18th instant, by Rev. W. W. Carothers, Mr. Noah Benfield and Miss Jane Thomasson, all of this District.

On Tuesday the 16th instant, by Rev. R. Y. Russell, Mr. Reuben McConnell Jr. of York District, and Miss Amanda J. McDonald of Chester District.

In this District on Thursday the 18th instant, by Rev. R. Y. Russell, Mr. John D. Anderson, and Miss Ianthe Jane, daughter of A. S. Wallace, Esq.

Died in this district on the 13th instant, Mr. Thomas G. Faris, in the 39th year of his age.

On the 19th instant, in Gaston county, N. C., J. Franklin, only son of Capt. E. M. Faris, in the 12th year of his age.

In Yorkville, on Monday last, 22d instant, Mary Flora, infant daughter of Mr. Jno. L. and Mrs. MaryMiller, aged 6 weeks and 2 days.

Issue of December 2, 1858

Died in this District on Monday morning last, 29th ult., Mr. John R. Wright, son of the late Dr. Samuel Wright, in the 21st year of his age.

Issue of December 23, 1858

Married in this District on the 15th instant, by John R. Wallace, Esq., Mr. William H. Fewell and Miss Catharine A., youngest daughter of J. T. & Elizabeth Foreman, all of this district.

Died in York District, on the 29th of November, John Randolph Wright, son of the late Dr. S. Wright, in the 21st year of his age....(eulogy)

Issue of January 6, 1859

Married on Tuesday, 21st ultimo, by Rev. J. R. Baird, Mr. J. N. Steeles, son of Mr. S. Steele, and Miss Martha J. Partlow, eldest daughter of Mr. James Partlow, all of this district.

Also, at the same time and place, by the same, Mr. G. E. M. Steele, son of Mr. A. Steele, and Miss Margaret M. Partlow, third daughter of Mr. James Partlow, all of this District.

on Tuesday evening, 21st ultimo, by Rev. W. W. Carothers, Mr. John H. Craig, and Miss Mary A., eldest daughter of David A. Jenkins, both of Gaston County, N. C.

On the 23d ultimo, by Rev. S. L. Watson, Mr. Wm. E. McCarter, and Miss A. J. Carothers, all of this District.

On Sunday evening, 26th ultimo, by James D. P. Currence, Esq., Mr. William G. Massey and Miss Pamela M. Wallace, both of Gaston County, N. C.

On Thursday evening, 18th ultimo, by Rev. W. W. Banks, Mr. R. W. Crawford, and Miss Sarah Jane, daughter of Mr. P. P. Ingraham, all of Chester District.

On Wednesday, 22nd ultimo, by John B. Jackson, Esq., Mr. Richard R. Strait, and Mrs. Mary McClean, all of this District.

On Tuesday evening, Dec. 28th,1858, by Rev. W. A. Gamewell, Rev. F. Asbury Wood and Miss Sue R. Logan.

On the 15th ultimo, by John Roddy, Esq., at the residence of the bride's mother, Mr. James M. McDowel, of York District, to Miss Margaret J. Ware, of Chester District.

On Tuesday, 23d ultimo, by John B. Jackson, Esq., Mr. Nicholas Roberts, and Miss Lucinda Jane, daughter of Mr. B. Steele Carson, all of this district.

Died near Concord Church, in this District, on Thursday morning, 30th ultimo, Mr. Thomas Faris, in the 84th year of his age.

On the 7th ultimo, in Lowndes County, Ms., Mrs. Harriet Gilmore, wife of James H. Gilmore, formerly of York District.

Issue of January 13, 1859

Married on Tuesday the 7th ultimo, in Walker County, Ala., by the Rev. J. A. Hill, Mr. J. A. May, and Miss J. P., daughter of W. P. and M. Y. Broach, all formerly of York District, S. C.

Also at the same place,on the 23d ultimo,by the Rev. J. A. Hill, Mr. J. W. Tram of Camden, S. C., and Miss M. M., daughter of W. P. and M. Y. Broach, formerly of York District, S. C.

On the 23d ult.,by John Roddey, Esq., Mr. John L. Hays and Miss Sarah E. Shillington, all of this district.

In Chester by the Rev. Wm. Curtis, D. D., at the residence of Rev. L. C. Hinton, Charles S. Brice, Esq., Editor of the Standard, and Miss Fannie Hinton.

On the evening of the 23d December, by Rev. W. W. Banks, Mr. Daniel Reid and Miss M. A., daughter of Mr. David Sexton.

Also, by the same, at 7 o'clock A. M., on the 29th Dec., Mr. M. Aldrich, and Miss A. M. C. Price, at the residence of her grandfather, James Yongue, Esq., all of Chester.

By Rev. E. W. Brice, on the evening of the 23d ult., at the house of David C. McWilliams, Mr. Robert Nelson and Miss Sarah McWilliams--all of Chester District.

On the evening of the 22d ult.,by Benj. W. Moore, Esq., Richard Wilson and Margaret Banks, all of Rocky Creek, Chester District.

Near Blairsville, by Abraham Gibson, Esq., at his residence, on the 23d ult., Calvin M. Gibson, and Miss Sarah Tongue, all of Chester District.

Died in Yorkville, S. C., on Wednesday evening, January 5th, Sarah Rebecca, only child of Asbury and Eliza C. Coward.

Issue of January 20, 1859

Married in Chester District on Thursday 6th instant, by Rev. L. McDonald, Mr. R. S. Lewis and Miss Martha J., daughter of D. G. Stinson, Esq.

In Yorkville, on Wednesday morning, 18th instant, by James Jefferys, Esq., Mr. John R. Alexander (Post Master) and Miss Mary, daughter of J. Leory Sutton, all of this District.

Issue of February 10, 1859

Married in this District on the 23d of December by A. Hardin, Esq., Mr. James S. Mullenax, and Miss Jane S. Collins,

On the 26th of December, by the same, Mr. Stephen White, and Miss Jane S. Hullender.

On the 29th of December, by the same, Mr. Alfred Conner, and Miss Jane Catharine Gladden, both of North Carolina.

On the 1st day of February, by the same, Mr. Alexander V. A. Wells and Miss Lucy Ann C. Blalock, both of North Carolina.

Issue of February 17, 1859

Married in Gaston county, N. C., on the 3d instant, by Rev. S. C. Pharr, D. D.,Mr. M. C. Abernathy and Miss Jane W., daughter of Capt. Jas. A. Henderson.

At Savannah, Georgia, in the Presbyterian Church, on the 27th ult., by Rev. David H. Porter, Mr. Edward C. McLure, of Chester, S. C., to Miss Lou, only daughter of Amzi Neely, Exq., of the former city.

On the 3d inst., by Rev. R. W. Brice, Mr. Wm. Estes, and Miss
Sarah, daughter of James Boyd, Sr., all of Chester District.
On Thursday, 20th ultimo, by Rev. J. R. Cassels, Mr. W. M.
Kennedy, of Chester, and Miss Rachel, daughter of John McGill, of
York District.
On Thursday morning, 3d instant, at the residence of Jas. Tur-
ner, Esq., by Rev. M. Pucket, Henry Pratt, and Miss Mary Turner,
all of Chester District.
On the 20th inst., by Rev. R. Y. Russell, Mr. Wm. A. Minter,
and Miss Cornelia M. Rosborough, all of York District.
Died in Chester District, on Wednesday, the 2d of February,
James B. H. Anderson,son of Dr. A. F. And Violet A. Anderson,
in the 4th year of his age....

Issue of February 24, 1859

Married in Yorkville, on Tuesday morning, 23d inst.,by Rev.
R. Y. Russell, Mr. Absolom Cody and Miss Ann, eldest daughter of
Thos. O'Farrell, all of this place.
On Tuesday the 10th inst., by J. D. F. Currence, Esq., Mr.
Joseph T. Forbes and Miss Clarissa A. Turner, all of this District.
In York District on the 21st instant, by Rev. J. J. Jones,
Mr. John White and Miss Francis Turner, all of Cleveland, N. C.
On the 10th instant, by Rev. R. W. Brice, Mr. William Caskey
and Miss Mary Jane, daughter of David E. McWilliams, all of
Chester District.
On the 2d instant, at the residence of Wm. Pratt, by Hiram
Steele, Esq., Mr. B. B. Wright and Miss Adaline, daughter of Wm.
Pratt, all of Chester.

Issue of March 3, 1859

Married on the 22d ultimo, by Rev. Saml. L. Watson, Mr. Wil-
liam A. Wilson, of Chester District, S. C., and Miss Mary E.
Linebarger of Gaston county, North Carolina.
On the 22d ultimo, by James D. P. Currence, Esq., Mr. James
W. Moore, of North Carolina and Miss Mary W. Smith, of York Dis-
trict.
On the 24th ultimo, by Rev. S. L. Watson, Mr. Thomas E. Har-
per and Miss Mary S. Dameron, all of York District.
On Thursday, 24th ultimo, by Jas. D. P. Currence, Esq., Mr.
Thomas H. Turner and Miss Susan D. Harper, all of York District.
In Hernando, Miss., on the 20th ultimo, by Rev. W. Y. Harris,
Mr. Charles L. Miller, formerly of York District, and Miss Eliza-
beth Morrow, of the former place.
On Thursday, 17th ultimo, by W. H. Anderson, Esq., Mr. John
W. Wilkes Jr., and Miss Martha K., daughter of Abner Wilkes, all
of Chester District.
On the 17th, Mr. Augustus P. Moffatt, of Troy, Tennessee ,
and Miss Jane, daughter of Samuel Lathan, of Fairfield District,
S. C.
On Thursday, 17th instant, Mr. Wesley Carter, and Miss Rhoda,
daughter of J. Wesley Wilkes, Esq., all of Chester District.

Issue of March 10, 1859

Married on the 24th ult., by Rev. James R. Baird, Mr. Thomas
C. Thomasson, of Mecklenburg, N. C., and Miss Harriet C. Fairies,
of this District.
Died at India Hood, York District, S. C.,on Sabbath night,

the 27th, Mr. Morrison Garrison, who was in the 24th year of his age...a member of the Methodist Church....

Issue of March 17, 1859

Married in Canton, Miss., on the 2d instant, by Rev. H. Sampson, Hon. Joseph H. Postell, formerly of York District, and Miss Betty C. Henderson, of the former place.

On Thursday, 10th instant, by Rev. S. L. Watson, Capt. Wm. T. Jackson, and Miss Margaret Rebecca, daughter of Capt. James and Mrs. Elizabeth Jackson, all of this District.

Died, Nancy Lester, wife of Phillip C. Lester, Esq., departed this life at Buena Vista, Greenville District, S. C., in the 65th year of her age, on Saturday, 5th instant. She leaves a husband and five children, one of whom is Rev. A. H. Lester, of the S. C. Conference, M. E. Church.

Issue of March 31, 1859

Married on Thursday 24th instant, by Rev. John S. Harris, Mr. R. Douglass Crawford and Miss C. J., daughter of S. J. H. Alexander, Esq., all of this District.

On Thursday evening, 24th instant, by Rev. W. W. Carothers, Mr. Barnett Cassels, of Chester District, and Miss Elizabeth M., daughter of the late James Wallace of this District.

In this District on the 22d instant, by Rev. Landy Wood, Mr. James D. Boyd, and Miss Jane, daughter of Joseph Starnes.

In this District on the 29th instant, by Wm. McGill, Esq., Mr. E. F. Bunch and Miss Margaret S. Inman, all of this District.

Issue of April 7, 1859

Married at the residence of the bride's father, in Walker county, Alabama, on the 10th ultimo, by Rev. J. A. Hill, Mr. J. J. Barnett and Miss E. Clarie, daughter of W. P. and M. Y. Broach, all formerly of York District.

On the 15th ult., by Thomas McGill, Esq., Mr. William J. Wilson, and Miss Faithy Hambright, all of this district.

On the 29th of March by Rev. A. A. James, Dr. Robert L. Love and Miss Jane Hemphill, all of York District.

Issue of April 14, 1859

Married on Thursday 7th instant, by Rev. S. L. Watson, Mr. Robert Jackson and Miss L. J. Hemphill, all of this District.

Died in this District on Friday, 1st instant, MaryJane, eldest daughter of Amos and Sarah Templeton, aged about 18 years.

Issue of April 21, 1859

Married near Bennettsville, on the 6th inst., by Rev. P. F. Kistler, P. B. McLaurin, Esq., to Miss Tommie J., daughter of T. C. Weatherly, Esq.

Issue of April 28, 1859

Married on Thursday 21st instant, by Rev. S. L. Watson, Mr. Richard G. Barnett, and Miss Elizabeth C. Hall, all of this District.

Died in Yorkville, on the 22d instant, Mr. John Parker, aged
about 61 years.
In this District on the 18th instant, Mr. Andrew O. Love,
aged about 21 years.
In Wappanucka, Arkansas, on the 19th ultimo, Lizzie, only
daughter of J. C. and F. J. McCarter, aged about two months.

Issue of May 5, 1859

Married on Tuesday, 26th ultimo, by Rev. J. R. Castles, Mr.
Robert A. Caldwell, of York District, and Miss Sarah, daughter
of Henry Castles, Esq., of Fairfield.
In this district, on the 26th ultimo, by Rev. Landy Wood, Mr.
P. T. Garrison, and Miss Mary Ann, daughter of Mr. Wm. Sturgis.
Died in this District on Wednesday evening, 27th ult., R. R.
Williamson, aged about 13 years.
In this District on Saturday, 30th ult., Mrs. Martha McMackin,
in the 73d year of her age.

Issue of May 12, 1859

Married on Tuesday evening, 10th instant, by Rev. S. C.
Miller, Rev. R. Lathan and Miss Fannie E., daughter of Dr. A. I.
Barron, all of Yorkville.
On Wednesday, 4th instant, by Rev. E. E. Boyce, Mr. Alexander
Glass, and Miss Margaret Barry, all of this District.
In Gaston County, N. C., on Sunday, 8th instant, by D. F. Reagan,
Esq., Mr. Thomas S. Wallace, of York District, and Miss Mary Jane
McKee, of the former place.
On Thursday, the 5th instant, by J. D. P. Currence, Esq.,
Mr. Moses A. Bigger and Miss Helen M. Campbell, all of this
District.
Died on Saturday the 16th day of April 1859, at the residence
of his parents, on Tabb street, in Petersburg, Va., John Starr
Lyon, infant son of John and Margaret M. Lyon, aged 8 months and
23 days.
In Yorkville, on Tuesday, 10th instant, Lucy Ann, infant
daughter of W. C. & E. A. Owen, aged 1 year, 1 month and 18 days.

Issue of May 19, 1859

Married on Thursday evening, May the 5th, by Rev. R. J. Boyd,
Charles W. Boyd, Esq., Associate Editor of the Unionville Times,
to Miss Maria Goudelock, second daughter of Davis Goudelock, Esq.,
of Unionville, S. C.

Issue of May 26, 1859

Married on Tuesday the 17th instant, by James D. P. Currence,
Esq., Mr. Henry Jones and Miss Margaret R. Eakins, all of this
District.
On Tuesday evening, 24th instant, by Rev. W. W. Carothers,
Mr. D. Marshal Campbell and Miss Mary J., daughter of Mr. Robert
Miller, all of this District.
Died in Mecklenburg County, N. C., May 18, 1849 (sic), Mrs.
R. O. McElhaney, daughter of Milton Neely, and wife of Randolph
H. McElhaney, in the 19th year of her age...member of
the Methodist Church....
Suddenly on the 21st instant, in Gaston County, N. C., Mrs.
Rhine, wife of Moses H. Rhine, Esq., leaving a devoted family....

Issue of June 2, 1859

Married on the 23d ultimo, by Rev. Drury Davis, Mr. George Quinn of York District, and Miss Genelia Putman, of Gaston County, N. C.

Died in Yorkville, on Thursday night last, 26th ultimo, Mr. J. Jackson Lowry, aged about 36 years.

Near Bethel, on the 14th ultimo, Mrs. Isabella, consort of Mr. J. Oates Moore, in the 56th year of her age.

Of Typhoid Fever, at Atlanta, Ga., on the 27th ultimo, Dr. J. D. Boyd, aged 57 years, 4 months and 25 days.

Died in Pope County, Ark., on the 10th ultimo of Typhoid Fever, Ezra D. Torrence...a native of Gaston County, N.C.... (eulogy)

Issue of June 9, 1859

Died in this District on the 1st instant, Mrs. Margaret Anders, aged about 22 years.

In this District on the 20th ultimo, James Thompson, infant son of P. and L. Garrison.

Issue of June 16, 1859

Died in Yorkville, on Friday last, 10th instant, Mrs. Elizabeth Beason, in the 56th year of her age.

Issue of June 23, 1859

Died at the residence of her brother, Thomas S. Erwin, on the 13th instant, Mrs. Jane S. Ross, wife of John M. Ross, Esq.,in the 20th year of her age.

In this District on Wednesday, 8th instant, Mr. John Rainey, aged about 76 years.

In this District on Thursday, 6th instant, Mrs. Nancy Meek, aged about 70 years.

Issue of June 30, 1859

Died at Davidson College, N. C., on the 14th of June last, of Flux, Mr. A. M. Barry, in the 30th year of his age...(eulogy)

Died in this place on Sabbath evening, 19th instant, Rev. William H. Johnston...born in Rowan County, N. C., 24th of May 1819. He was a graduate of Davidson College, and of the Princeton Theological Seminary; license by the Presbytery of New Brunswick, April 1845...left wife and three little daughters....

In this District on the 21st instant, Mrs. Sarah Henderson, aged 75 years. The deceased was one of the victims of the storm on the 15th of last month, and died from injuries received at that time.

In Unionville, on the morning of the 21st inst., a 1 o'clock, the only son of Geo. L. and E. M. Pratt, aged 11 months and 22 days.

Issue of July 7, 1859

Married in Yorkville on Sunday evening, 3d instant, by James Jefferys, Esq., Mr. George Williams and Miss Elizabeth Holbrooks, all of this place.

In Gaston county, N. C.,on the 30th ultimo , by Rev. Davidson Hall, Mr. S. Henry Williams, of Yorkville, and Miss M. J. Hand, of the former place.

Also, at the same time and place, by the same, Mr. L. H. Ford, and Miss L. M. Hand, all of Gaston.

Issue of July 14, 1859

Married on Thursday, 7th instant, by C. A. Huffstetler, Esq., Mr. M. Chambers Workman and Miss Nancy J. McColloch, all of Gaston County, N. C.

Died in Union District, of Typhoid Fever, on the 4th instant, Mr. William T. Smith, in the 39th year of his age.

Issue of July 21, 1859

Married on Thursday evening, the 14th instant, by Rev. W. W. Carothers, Mr. John M. Sourney, of Ireland, and Miss Nancy Reeves, of this District.

Issue of July 28, 1859

Married on Thursday, 16th day of June, by J. P. Hood, Esq., Mr. Gilham Minter, and Miss Amanda Stewart, all of York District.

By the same, at Hood's Factory, on Tuesday, 12th inst., Mr. J. G. Latham, and Miss Rachel Latham, all of the same District.

By the same, and at the same place, on Thursday, 21st instant, James Feemster, of York, and Miss Winney Mitchell, of Chester.

Issue of August 4, 1859

Married on Thursday 7th of July, by A. Hardin, Esq., Mr. Jerome White and Miss Eliza Roark, all this District.

On the 25th ultimo, by the same, Mr. George S. Pool, and Mrs. Martha Ann Young, both of Cleveland county, N. C.

On the 28th ultimo, by the same, Maj. Marcus H. Bird and Miss Amanda Moore, all of York District.

IN "Benton" on the 28th ultimo, by J. P. Hood, Esq., Mr. William McLean, and Miss Mary S. Montgomery, all of this District.

Died in this District, on the 1st instant, Mrs. Elizabeth Boyd, wife of the late David Boyd.

Near Hickory Grove, in this District on Thursday, 19th ultimo, Mrs. Margaret Whitesides, wife of Thomas Whitesides, and daughter of Wm. Berry, Esq.

Issue of August 11, 1859

Married on the 28th ultimo, by James Jefferys, Esq., Mr. Andrew Jackson Mitchem and Miss Elizabeth White, all of this District.

Issue of August 18, 1859

Married on the 11th instant, by Rev. J. A. Davies, Mr. Rufus J. Whitesides, and Miss Eliza Ann, eldest daughter of Mr. R. Jackson Brown, all of this District.

On the 11th instant, by Rev. S. L. Watson, Mr. B. F. Brown, of Mecklenburg, N. C., and Miss Susan M. Brown, of York District.

Departed this life in Yorkville, on the evening of the 15th instant, Mrs. Harriet Creps, wife of Mr. Wesley Creps, in her 22d year...member of the Methodist Episcopal Church....

In Yorkville on the 8th instant, Miss Eleanor Isabella, second
daughter of James M. & Lucinda Partlow, aged 17 years and two
months.

Died on Sabbath, the 24th of July last, at the residence of
her mother, in Gaston County, N. C., Mrs. Catharine Garvin, in the
36th year of her age...daughter of Col. J. Holland, and his wife
Elizabeth Holland, residing in Gaston County, N. C., where she
was born and reared...marriage with Dr. JohnRatchford, of York
District, S. C...transfered her membership to the Independent
Presbyterian Church, of which Dr. Ratchford was a member. In the
year 1853, Dr. Ratchford died, and in 1857, Mrs. Ratchford married
Col. W. W. Garvin, of Barnwell, S. C....(eulogy)

Issue of August 25, 1859

Died near Tulip, Dallas county, Arkansas, on the 24th ultimo,
Mrs. Frances Louisa (formerly Miss White) consort of B. F.
Harville, in the 22d year of her age...member of the Presbyterian
Church for about 6 years--first at Unity, in York District, S. C.,
and at Tulip, Arkansas....leaves a husband, and brothers and sis-
ters....

Issue of September 1, 1859

Married at Ebenezer, York District,on the 25th ultimo, by
Rev. T. W. Hall, Mr. William Starr, and Miss Euphemia Murphy,
all of York.

On the 18th ultimo, by Rev. M. Pucket, Mr. A. N. McNinch, of
Chester, and Miss Amanda H., daughter of Allen G. and Martha
Lawrence, of York.

Issue of September 8, 1859

Married in Drew County, Arkansas, on the 16th ultimo, by Rev.
J.W. Carr, Dr. D. H. Thomasson, late of Yorkville, S. C., ad
Miss C. Bell, of the former place.

August 16th, by Rev. A. A. James, Mr. Matthew S. Lynn, of
York District, and Mrs. Jane C. Goudelock, of Union District.

On the 30th ultimo, by J. D. P. Currence, Esq., Mr. Doctor
A. Whitaker, and Miss Matilda J. Wallace, all of this District.

Died in this District, on Monday, 5th instant, Mrs. Nancy
Jane, wife of Alexander Wylie, aged 25 years.

Issue of September 15, 1859

Married in Lancaster District, on the 31st ult., Thomas B.
Withers, Esq., of Fort Mills, York District, and Miss Martha J.,
daughter of Adam Ivey, Esq.

On the 13th instant, by James Jefferys, Esq., Mr. John W.
Lilly, and Miss Harriet C. Dobson, all of this District.

Issue of September 22, 1859

Married in Cleveland co., N. C., on the 8th instant, by Rev.
W. S. Black, Mr. Wm. Ellis, of York District, S. C., to Miss
Nancy J. Bell, of the former place.

Onthe 13th instant, by Rev. J. A. Davies, Mr. J. Meek Mc-
Elwee, and Miss Margaret Ann, second daughter of Mr. James Caldwell, all of this District.

Died in this District of Consumption, on Saturday, 17th instant, Mrs. Isabella Smith, consort of James A. Smith, aged about 50 years.

Issue of September 29, 1859

Married on the 15th inst., by the Rev. R. Lathan, Mr. W. A. Barron, to Miss Eliza Hammond, all of this District.
Died in this District on Sunday evening, 25th instant, Winslow A., youngest son of W. B. and Lucinda Traylor, aged 16 years and 11 months, leaving a disconsolate father and two sisters....

Issue of October 6, 1859

Married on Thursday 29th ultimo, by Rev. W. W. Carothers, Mr. John G. Ferguson, and Miss Rhoda L., second daughter of J. E. and E. Grist, all of Yorkville.
In Williamson county, Texas, at the residence of the bride's father, by Rev. W. M. Overstreet, Mr. A. S. Mason and Miss Maggie daughter of Col. S. D. Carothers.
On the 25th ultimo, by E. M. Carpenter, Esq., Mr. John J. McCosh, of York District, and Miss S. O. Long, of Rutherford County, N. C.
Died in this District on Monday, 3d instant, Columbus, eldest son of Mr. Franklin Miller, in the 16th year of his age.
In Yorkville, on the 4th instant, Martha McConnell, youngest daughter of Jerome C. and Martha E. Miller, aged 1 year, 11 months and 26 days.

Issue of October 13, 1859

Married on Tuesday 11th instant, by Rev. J. M. H. Adams, Mr. Charles R. Moore of Yorkville, S. C., and Miss Mary J. Gregory, formerly of Clarksville, Virginia.
At the Episcopal Church in Yorkville, on Tuesday evening, 11th instant, by Rev. A. F. Olmstead, Mr. S. Banks Meacham, and Miss Mary Henley, step-daughter of Mr. B. T. Wheeler, all of this place.
On the 4th instant, by Rev. Mr. Bonner, Mr. Marion Moore and Miss Martha Guntharp, all of this District.
On the 6th instant, by J. D. P. Currence, Esq., Mr. William S. Barnett, and Miss Sarah E. Whitesides, all of this district.
On the 6th instant, by Daniel Ragan, Esq., Mr. R. A. H. Neagle and Miss Isabella Falls, all of Gaston County, North Carolina.
At the residence of the bride's mother, on the 6th instant, by Rev. W. W. Carothers, Mr. David M. Walker, formerly of York District, and Miss Rosa Ann Falls, of Gaston county, North Carolina.

Issue of October 20, 1859

Married on Tuesday 18th instant, by James Jefferys, Esq., Mr. Adolphus Doster, and Miss Elizabeth Jane, daughter of James & Sarah Alexander, all of this District.
At the house of E. C. Chambers, Esq., in Cleveland county, N. C., on the 11th instant, by Rev. W. C. Patterson, Mr. J. J. M. Heath, and Miss Hester C. Patterson.
At the same time and place, by the same, Mr. Robert H. Porter, Esq., of Lancaster District, and Miss Laura C. Patterson, late of Georgia.
Died in this District on the 6th inst., Mrs. Elizabeth F., wife of Mr. James T. Foreman, aged about 53 years...left a husband,

several children and many friends....

Issue of October 27, 1859

Married on the 16th instant, at the residence of Mrs. Mary Duff, by J. D. P. Currence, Esq., Mr.Andrew J. Martin, and Miss Mary M. Dameron, all of Gaston County, N. C.

Died on Monday, 17th instant, infatn daughter of Capt. James and Elizabeth Jackson, aged 3 weeks.

Issue of November 10, 1859

Married in Gaston County, N. C., on the 12th ultimo, by Rev. Mr. Peterson, Mr. William Sams, and Miss A. E. Martin.

Also, on the 13th ult., by Rev.J. D. Hall, Mr. A. F. W. Dixon, and Miss M. R. Ratchford, all of Gaston County, N. C.

On the evening of the 25th ultimo, by Rev. J. S. Harris, at the house of Mrs. Joseph Poag, of York District, Mr. Edward H. Stringfellow, of Chester District, and Mrs. Margaret Miller.

Died in this District, on the 3d instant, Lois Ann, daughter of Joseph and Mary Thomas, in the 16th year of her age.

Near Ebenezer, in this District, on the 14th ultimo, Mrs. Elizabeth Henderson, in the 58th year of her age.

Issue of November 17, 1859

Married in Gaston County, N. C., on the 1st inst., by J. F. Smyer, Esq., Mr. Thos Ford, and Miss Sarah Kendrick.

On the 1st inst., by James Quinn, Esq., Mr. Wm. Motin, and Miss Margaret A. Johnston.

On the 8th inst., by Rev. L. Wood, Mr. Jos. H. Cathcart, and Miss Sarah E., daughter of John Garrison, all of York District.

In this District, on the 15th. inst., by Rev. L. Wood, Mr. John H. Caton and Miss Sarah Jane, daughter of Mark Garrison.

Issue of November 24, 1859

Married on the 10th instant, by Rev. S. L. Watson, Mr. Peyton B. Currence to Miss Sarah C. Boyd, all this District.

On the 15th instant, by the same, Mr. James L. Bigger, and Miss Violet P. Partlow, all of this District.

Died in Yorkville, on the 15th instant, at the residence of Capt. J. C. Phillips, Martha A. E., daughter of Mr. A. B. Bigger, of Crowder's Creek, aged seven years, five months and nineteen days.

At the residence of her father in York District, on the 9th instant, Martha Antoinette, daughter of John and Ann Hall, aged two years and 25 days.

Issue of December 1, 1859

Married on the 25th ultimo, by John R. Logan, Esq., Thomas P. McGill, Esq., of Gaston County, N. C., and Mrs. Elizabeth Fulton, of Cleveland county, N. C.

Issue of December 8, 1859

Died in this District on the 11th ult., Mary E. J., daughter of S. A. and M. J. Faris, aged 13 months.

In this District, on the 24th ultimo, William Harvey, son of

S. A. and M. J. Faris, in the 5th year of his age.
   In this District, on the 21st ultimo, James Boyd, Esq., aged
about 50 years.
   Married on the 1st instant, by the Rev'd Wm. T. Hall, Mr.
William J. Kimbrell, to Miss Margaret, daughter of N. A. Steele,
Esq., all of York District.
   On Wednesday 30th ultimo, by Rev. Wade Hill, Mr. Charles E.
Betchler, of Spartanburg, and Miss Jane L., eldest daughter of Mr.
James Wylie, of York District.
   On the 24th ultimo, by Rev. Mr. Lindsay, Mr. Wm. G. G. Postell,
of Yorkville, and Miss Anna McCaslan, daughter of Mr. W. W. Mc-
Caslan, of Abbeville.

Issue of December 15, 1859

   Married at the residence of the bride's father, York District,
S. C., on Wednesday, 6 o'clock p. m., Nov. 39th, 1859 by Rev.
Wade Hill, of North Carolina, Rev. Chas. E. Bechtler, formerly
of Spartanburg, S. C., late of York Dist., S. C., (eldest son of
Christopher Bechtler, Esq. of Spartanburg, S. C., so widely known
for his workmanship in gold and watches; also the associate
founder of the "Bechtler coin,") to Miss Jennie L., second daughter
of James Wylie, Esq., of York Dist., S. C.
   On the 1st instant, by Rev. J. C. Williams, W. L. Hudgens,
Esq., of Laurens, to Miss Corrie Klugh, of Cokesbury, Abbeville,
S. C.
   Died at Laurensville, S. C., on Saturday, 3d instant, Eugene
oldest son of P. D. and E. N. Elliott--a little boy about two
years old....
   In this District on the 6th instant, Mr. J. D. Lathem, aged
about 35 years.
   In this District on the 6th instant, Miss Jane Hartness,
aged about 12 years.
   In this District of Typhoid Fever, on the 6th ultimo, Elwin
F. B., son of Elias and Mary Jackson, in teh 20th year of his age.
   In Harris County, Georgia of Dropsy, on the 3d ultimo, John
Alexander, in the 50th year of his age.
   At the residence of her husband, in Ouachita County, Arkansas,
on the 10th of November, Mrs. Martha Ann, wife of Dr. Isaac Hawkins,
and daughter of John G. Gill--in the 32d year of her age.

Issue of December 22, 1859

   Married on Thursday 1st instant, by Rev. R. Y. Russell, Maj.
Robert L. Lindsay, and Miss Jane, daughter of Thomas C. Burris,
all of this District.
   On the 15th instant, by Rev. J. M. Anderson, Mr. David A. A.
Watson, and Miss Margaret L. Tate, all of this District.
   On the 15th instant, by Rev. S. L. Watson, Mr. Wm. Thomas
Barry, and Mary J. Pierce, all of this District.
   In Yorkville, on Thursday, 8th instant, by Rev. W. T. Hall,
Mr. John C. Holly, of Fairfield District, and Miss Mary, daughter
of Wylie L. Harris, Esq., of this place.
   On Tuesday 20th inst., by Maurice A. Moore, Esq., Mr. Thomas
Freeman and Miss Margaret E. Creighton, all of this District.
   Died on Wednesday the 14th inst., at McConnellsville, Mr.
Reuben McConnell, in the 61st year of his age. (eulogy)...left a
wife and three sons.
   In Yorkville, on the 16th inst.,Julia, youngest child of Col.
S. N. and Mrs. M. M. Stowe, aged 14 months and 15 days....

Issue of January 5, 1860

Married in Jefferson County, Alabama, on the 21st ultimo, by Rev. Thos. J. Davidson, Mr. William E. Murphy, formerly of York-ville, S. C., and Miss Florence M. Burford, of the former place.

On the 22d ultimo, by Rev. R. Y. Russel, Mr. W. P. Hobbs, and Miss Kate O'Leary, all of this place.

On the 29th ultimo, by A. S. Wallace, Esq., Mr. R. G. Bratton, and Miss Sarah Smith, all of this District.

On the 29th ultimo, by D. F. Reagan, S. R. Ewing, and Miss Mary Ann Long--all of Gaston, N. C.

On the 22d ultimo, by James Jefferys, Magistrate, Mr. Thaddeus R. Bates, and Miss Nancy C. Rawls, all of this District.

On the 27th December, at Anderson C. H., by the Rev. A. A. Moore, Mr. T. J. Glover, of Orangeburg, and Miss Toccoa, daughter of Judge J. N. Whitner.

On the 3d instant, by the Rev. Dr. O'Connell, Mr. Joseph Fried-eberg, to Mrs. M. A. H. Thorn.

Issue of January 12, 1860

Married in Chester District on the 20th ultimo, Mr. G. F. Bowler, and Miss Margaret Bruce.

In Chester District, on the 29th ultimo, Mr. John Harrison, and Miss Juliana Collins, daughter of John Collins.

At Rich Hill, Chester District, on the 29th ultimo, Mr. John L. McCorkle, and Miss Rebecca Lock, both of York District.

In Chester District, on the 3d instant, by Rev. L. C. Hinton, Mr. Elias Smith, and Miss Francis Cook.

On Tuesday Dec. 20th by the Rev. Mr. Smith, Mr. Austin Saville, of Mecklenburg, N. C., to Miss Jane Harper, of York District, S. C.

On Wednesday, 21st December, by B. J. Patterson, Esq., Mr. R. H. Fullwood, of Fort Mills, to Miss Francis E. Harris, of York District.

Also, on the same day, Mr. Newton Johnston, and Miss Josephine Harris, all of York District.

On the 22d ultimo, by A. F. Love, Esq., Mr. O. L. Wallace, and Miss M. C. Sherer, all of York District.

On Thursday, the 5th instant, by J. R. Wallace, Esq., Mr. J. J. Nivens, and Miss Martha Adkins, all of this District.

Died at Fort Mills, York District, S. C., on Monday, the 2nd instant, Mrs. Margaret Amelia, wife of B. F. Powell, aged 30 years....

Issue of January 19, 1860

Married in Yorkville, on Tuesday morning, 17th instant, by Rev. L. A. Johnston, Mr. Sample Alexander, of Chester, and Miss Lucie H. Clawson, of this place.

In Holmes county, Miss., on the 20th ultimo, by Rev. Mr. Rayner, Mr. William White and Miss Lizzie Roach, both formerly of Chester District.

In Chester District, on the 22d ultimo, Mr. Robert Fannel and Miss Mary Lynn.

On the 22d ultimo, by Geo. L. McNeel, Esq., Mr. John Robinson, and Miss Mary Barnedore, all of Chester District.

At Chester Court House, on the 10th instant, by Rev. A. G. Stacy, Mr. C. E. Simms of Columbia, to Mrs. Sarah Pinchback of the former place.

In Chester, on Tuesday of last week, Mr. Wm. Cornwell and Miss
Sallie Walker, all of that place.
    On the 11th instant, at the Central House, in Columbia, by Rev.
J. M. C. Breaker, Mr. Wm. Richard White of Charleston, S. C., to
Miss Elizabeth Jane Carroll, of the former place.
    In Mecklenburg County, N. C., on the 27th ultimo, Mr. John
Hanna, and Miss Mary Carothers.
    Died near Ebenezerville, on the 9th instant, Mr. James P.
Hutchinson, aged about 52 years. The deceased leaves a widow
and two children....

Issue of January 26, 1860

    Married on Tuesday 10th instant, by Rev. E. Lindsay, Mr. John
McCants of Yorkville, and Mrs. M. C. Monroe of Laurens District.
    In Chester District, on Sunday, 15th instant, Miss Mary
Jane Lee, and Mr. James H. Grant.
    In Chester District, on the 12th instant, by Geo. L. McNiel
Esq., Mr. Robert Bell and Miss Margaret Barens.

Issue of February 2, 1860

    Married in Canton, Miss., at the residence of Benjamin Cham-
bers, Esq., on Wednesday morning, 18th ultimo, by Dr. Light, Mr.
Chas. Thompson of Kentucky, and Miss Harriet D. Chambers, of
Canton.

Issue of February 9, 1860

    Died in Newnan, Georgia, on the 26th ultimo, Miles G. Simril,
formerly of Yorkville, in the 50th year of his age.

Issue of February 16, 1860

    Married on the 9th instant, by Maurice A. Moore, Esq., Mr.
Thomas Swords and Miss Elizabeth Neely, all of Rock Hill.
    On the 2nd instant, by J. D. P. Currence, Esq., Mr. Franklin
H. Youngblood and Miss Elvira J. Burns, all of this District.
    On the 7th instant, by Rev. S. L. Watson, Mr. David W. Barron,
to Miss Sarah J. C. Tate, all of this District.
    On the evening of the 14th, at the residence of the bride's
father, by Rev. J. M. H. Adams, Mr. John J. Smith, and Miss Jane,
daughter of Wm. P. and Amelia McFadden, all of Yorkville.
    Died in Cleveland County, N. C., on Tuesday, February 7th,
1860, Langdon Cheves, son of Rufus and Martha Roberts, aged 11
months and 19 days....
    In this District on the 29th ult., of Puerperal Convulsions,
Mrs. Margaret, wife of E. T. Faris.
    On Saturday, 4th instant, Mrs. Mary M. Hunter, relict of the
late Dr. John B. Hunter, in the 46th year of her age.

Issue of February 23, 1860

    Married on Thursday, 16th instant, by Rev. J. A. Davies, Mr.
Wm. M. Caldwell, and Miss S. E., daughter of G. F. And H. B.
Ferguson, all of this District.
    On Thursday, 9th instant, by Wm. McGill, Esq., Franklin
Purseley and Miss Emily Quinn, all of York District.
    On Tuesday, 14th instant, by John Roddy, Esq., Mr. John T.
Boyd, and Miss N. Caroline Wylie, all of this District.

In Orange Parish, at the residence of the bride, by Rev. A. B. Stevens, on Tuesday, 14th inst., Mr. Jno. L. Carrol, of the "Central House," Columbia, and Mrs. Sarah E. Culler.

Issue of March 1, 1860

Married on the evening of the 16th of February, by Rev. H. H. Spann, George Adolphus Fink, Esq., formerly of Salisbury, N. C., now editor of the Lexington (S. C.) Flag, and Miss L. H. daughter of the Rev. H. A. Smith, local minister of the Methodist Episcopal Church, South.

In Chester, at the "Rail Road Hotel," on Tuesday, 28th ultimo, by W. H. Anderson, Esq., Mr. E. Bennett, and Miss Tabitha Knott of Forsyth County, N. C.

Died in this District on the 17th instant, of Pneumonia, Miss Amanda, eldest daughter of John C. and Amanda M. Wilson, in the 20th year of her age....

Died on the 24th ult., at her residence near Bethel, Mrs. Deborah Watson, relict of Samuel Watson, deceasd. aged 92 years.

Howard Hayne Caldwell was born in the village of Newberry, S. C., Tuesday the 20th of Sept...married Miss Montague in 1857, and pursued his profession in Mobile, Ala...died in Columbia, 21 Feb. 1860. (eulogy and account).

Issue of March 8, 1860

Married on the 1st instant, by Rev. R. A. Ross, Mr. Wm. H. Lindsay, and Miss Mary R., eldest daughter of John M. and Margaret A. Brison, all of this District.

In Chester, on the evening of the 28th of February, by Rev. Mr. White, Dr. J. S. Pride and Miss Phoeba A., daughter of the late Thos. McLure.

Died Near Yorkville, on Friday, 3d instant, Mrs. Holly Murphy, aged 52 years.

In this District, on the 29th ult., Mr. James R. Williams, in the 78th year of his age...for the last forty years a consistent member of the Presbyterian Church.

In this District on the 26th ult., Alice, infant daughter of Perry and Sarah Jane Martin, aged 3 weeks....

Issue of March 15, 1860

Married on the 8th instant, at the residence of the bride's father, in Gaston County, N. C., by James Quinn, Esq., Mr. J. L. Quinn, and Miss Annette Bradley.

Ey Wm. McGill, Esq., at his residence on the 8th instant, Mr. James Neely and Miss Sarah Robison, all of this District.

On the 1st of March, at the residence of M. C. Heath, Esq., in Lancaster District, S. C., by Rev. Mr. Brown, Mr. J. P. Heath, of Charlotte, N. C., and Miss Louisa Stewart, of York District, S. C.

Died at Rock Hill, on Sunday morning last, Mrs. Mary S., wife of A. E. Hutchinson, Esq.

At his residence in Gaston county, N. C., on the 12th instant, Mr. Thomas Groves, aged about 93 years.

In this District on Tuesday, 13th instant, Miss Jane Campbell, in the 83rd year of her age.

In Yorkville, on Monday, 12th instant, Mrs. Mary Jane, wife of W. Dickson Miller, in the 36th year of her age.

Issue of March 22, 1860

Married in Yorkville on the 11th instant, by James Jefferys, Magistrate, Mr. William B. Williams, and Miss Mary E. Holdbrooks.
Died in Yorkville on the 17th instant, Mrs. Amelia H., wife of W. P. McFadden, aged 53 years.
In this District, on the 7th instant, Mary Jane, infant daughter of John and Frances Parrot, aged about 8 months.

Issue of March 29, 1860

Married on the 20th instant, at the residence of the bride's father, By Rev. J. D. Hall, Mr. R. G. C. Love, and Miss Susan E. Rhyne, all of Gaston County, N. C.
Died in Yorkville, on the 23rd instant, Mrs. Margaret Carson, in the 42nd year of her age.
In Drew County, Arkansas, on the 6th instant, Joseph M. Boggs, formerly of York District, in the 40th year of his age.

Issue of April 5, 1860

Died in this District, on the 19th ult., Mrs. Jane Hopper, wife of H. P. Hopper, aged twenty six years....
In this District, on the 29th ult., Mr. John Warren, aged 83 years.
In Nashville, Tenn., on the 2d of October, 1858, Mr. G. G. Durham, formerly of this District, aged about 72 years.
In Prairie county, Arkansas, of flux, on the 6th ult., Mrs. Sarah E. Smith, consort of Mijamin Smith, formerly of this District.

Issue of April 12, 1860

Died April 10th, Prof. R. K. Thomas, in the twenty-second year of his age...graduated with distinction at the Citadel Academy, at the early age of nineteen, he connected himself with the King's Mountain Military School....
Died in this District on the 31st ult., Mr. Robert N. Kennedy, aged about 19 years.
In this District, on the 1st instant, Mr. Hiram Clark, aged about 30 years.
In this District on the 8th instant, Benjamin Davis, aged about 45 years.
In this District on the 4th instant, Mrs. Cynthia Hill, in the 61st year of her age.

Issue of April 19, 1860

Married in Yorkville, on Tuesday evening, the 17th instant, by Rev. W. W. Carothers, Rev. W. W. Ratchford, of Gaston County, N. C., and Miss Mary C., youngest daughter of Thos. H. and Jailey Smith, of this place.
In this District on Thursday evening, the 12th instant, by James Jefferys, Magistarte, Mr. William M. Collins, and Miss Emily S. Wilson, all of this District.
Died in this District, on the 10th instant, Mr. Jesse K. Armstrong, in the 63d year of his age.

Issue of April 26, 1860

Died in Bethel, York District, S. C., at the residence of
Joseph Adams, on the 18th instant, Mrs. Jane M. McLean, wife of
Gen. R. D. S. McLean, dec'd, aged 58 years...her father, Joseph
Adams....

Issue of May 3, 1860

Died at his residence in Bethel, in this District on the 25th
ult., Mr. Joseph Adams, aged 77 years and 2 months...a Ruling
Elder for nearly fifty years. (eulogy)
Near Indiahook Church, on the 10th ultimo, Mrs. Ann Garrison,
aged about 83 years.
Near Fort Mills, on the 13th ultimo, Mrs. Rebecca, consort
of Mr. S. A. Harris.
At Ebenezer, on the 17th ultimo, Laddie H., son of S. M. and
M. J. Mills, aged about 18 months.

Issue of May 10, 1860

Married on the 1st of May, by Rev. L. A. Johnson, Mr. E.
Jackson West, of Chester, and Miss Lizzie E., daughter of James
and E. H. Jefferys, of Yorkville.
Died in Yorkville, on Sunday, 6th instant, Mrs. Elizabeth
Herndon, in the 76th year of her age.

Issue of May 24, 1860

Married on Thursday 17th inst., by Rev. S. L. Watson, Mr.
R. P. Jackson and Miss Emily J. Currence, all of this District.
On the 17th instant, by J. D. P. Currence, Esq., Ephraim A.
Massey and Miss Mary Ann Elmore, all of Gaston County, N. C.
Died in Bradley County, Ark., at the residence of T. A. Richard-
son, on the 24th ultimo, Miss Elizabeth Strain, formerly of
York District, aged 31 years, 11 months and 21 days....
At his residence in this District, on Monday, 21st instant,
Mr. John Smith, of Bethel, in the 85th year of his age.

Issue of May 31, 1860

Married in Fairfield District on the 15th instant, Dr. John
Boyd, and Miss Lucy Bryan, all of Fairfield.
Died near Fort Mills, on the 17th instant, Mrs. Catharine
M., wife of T. G. Culp, aged 26 years.

Issue of June 7, 1860

Died in Yorkville, on the 17th ultimo, Mrs. Amanda M., wife
of Mr. Zachariah Howell, in the 25th year of her age.

Issue of June 14, 1860

Married in this District on the 5th instant, by Rev. John S.
Harris, Mr. Wm. Smart, of Rutherford county, N. C., and Miss M.
E. Murphy, of the former place.

Issue of June 21, 1860

Married on the 31st ultimo, at Wm. T. Robinson's, by J. P. Hood, Esq., Mr. Joseph Feemster, and Mrs. Amarinta Galloway.

On the 7th instant, at William J. Wilson's, by J. P. Hood, Esq., Mr. Nathaniel Hill and Miss Jane, eldest daughter of Isaac and Vina Minter, all of this district.

Died in Yorkville, on the 12th instant, Mrs. Lucinda Partlow, in the 42d year of her age.

In this district, on the 12th instant, Mr. Vincent Parks, in the 51st year of his age.

At Landsford, Chester District, on the 31st ultimo, Mrs. Caroline V. Perry, in the 31st year of her age....

Issue of June 28, 1860

Married in Chester, on the 6th instant, at the residence of J. L. Albright, by Rev. A. G. Stacey, Mr. G. A. Albright, and Miss Amanda, daughter of O. P. and Harriet Farrar.

Issue of July 5, 1860

Died near Olney, in Gaston County, N. C., at the residence of Nathan Mendenhall, on the 1st instant, Mrs. Martha C. Torrence, consort of John Torrence, in the 89th year of her age.

In this District, on the 25th ultimo, Miss Martha Love, aged about 80 years.

In this District on the 28th ultimo, Mrs. Esther Bigger, in the 73d year of her age.

In this District, on the 2nd instant, Mr. A. P. Quinn, aged about 24 years.

Issue of July 12, 1860

Died in this District, on Wednesday, 20th ultimo, Laura Matilda, daughter of Capt. John J. and Mrs. N. J. Wylie, aged one month and eleven days....

Died in his carriage, on his way from Charlotte to his residence in York District, on the 6th inst., Mr. S. A. Faris, in the 41st year of his age.

In this District on the 30th ult., Mrs. M. M. J. Boyd, wife of T. E. W. Boyd, in the 22d year of her age.

In this District, on the 4th instant, at the residence of her son, J. A. Laney, Esq., Mrs. Hannah Laney, in the 77th year of her age.

In Cherokee county, Ala., Sunday, June 4, Abram Stanhope, son of A. P. and M. E. Heggins, formerly of York District.

Issue of July 19, 1860

Married on Tuesday morning, 17th instant, by Rev. R. Y. Russell, Mr. J.A. Carrol, and Miss Sarah James, daughter of Mrs. Arabella James, all of Yorkville.

Died in this district on the 12th instant, Mr. Allen G. Lawrence, in the 49th year of his age.

In Charlotte, N. C., on the 2d instant, of Typhoid Fever, Mrs. Jane E. Whitener, in the 28th year of her age-- wife of H. H. Whitener, and daughter of John B. and Eliza Adams, of York District.

YORKVILLE ENQUIRER

Issue of July 26, 1860

Married in this District, on the 15th inst., by G. W. Cobb,
Esq., Mr. D. Crocket Ramsey, and Miss Martha Childers, all of
this District.
Died in Chester, on the 17th instant, Mrs. Elizabeth Owens,
consort of J. T. Owens, in the 24th year of her age.
In this District, near Howell's Ferry, on the 14th instant,
Mr. Vines C. Smith.
In this District, on the 13th instant, Miss Ruga Leech.

Issue of August 2, 1860

Died at Pleasant Ridge, Gaston Co., N. C., on Tuesday, 24th
inst., of Quinsey, Benjamin, son of David A. and Lodema Jenkins,
age about five years.

Issue of August 9, 1860

Married in this District on the 26th ultimo, by J. D. P.
Currence, Esq., Mr. R. R. Phelan and Mrs. Charlotte L. McQuinn,
all of Mecklenburg, N. C.
On the 1st inst., by Wm. McGill, Esq., Mr. Robert A. Jackson,
and Miss Sarah C. McCarter, all of this district.
At Rose's Hotel, on Sunday evening, the 29th ultimo, by
Rev. L. A. Johnson, Mr. Sylvanus Simmons, and Miss Mary Clinton,
eldest daughter of the late Jesse Armstrong, all of this District.

Issue of August 16, 1860

Married by Rev. J. I. Bonner, on the morning of the 9th instant,
at sunrise, in the village of Due West, S. C., Mr. Thomas N. Pol-
hill, of the Louisville (Ga.) *Gazette*, and Miss Josephine Hawthorn,
for the former place.
On the 7th instant, by Rev. Jno S. Harris, Mr. John Doby Williamson, of Chester District, and Miss Mary E., daughter of Samuel
Rainey, Esq., of York District, S. C.
In Charlotte, N. C., at the residence of A. C. Steele, Esq.,
on the 2nd instant, by Rev. R. Y. Russell, Mr. Baxter H. Moore,
of Yorkville, S. C., and Miss C. E. Biles, of the former place.

Issue of August 23, 1860

Married on the 16th instant, by Rev. J. B. Watt, Col. W. H.
McCorkle, of Yorkville, S. C., and Mrs. Elva M. Dixon, of
Mecklenburg county, N. C.
On Thursday evening, the 9th instant, by J. W. Smith, Esq.,
Mr. Jasper Ragan, and Miss Elmina Pierce, all of Gaston County,
N. C.
On Tuesday evening, the 21st instant, by Rev. W. W. Carothers,
Mr. A. L. Henderson and Miss Martha P., daughter of Mr. Robert H.
Craig, all of Gaston County, N. C.

Issue of August 30, 1860

Died in York District, S. C., on the 16th of June, Rev. John
Leroy Davies, in the 61st year of his age...eldest son of Rev.
John B. and brother of Rev. Wm. B. Davies, both of whom predeceased
him...pastor of Catholic Church on Rocky Creek, Chester District...
first married to Miss Isabella, daughter of John Hemphill, M.D.,

of Chester District. His second wife was the daughter of Rev.
S. B. Wilson, D. D., of the Union Theological Seminary, Va. Rev.
Samuel W. Davies of Pecan Grove, La. (his eldest son) and seven
others survive...(long account)
    At Micanopy, Fla., on the 27th ultimo, Mr. J. P. Garrison,
formerly of York District, aged 45 years.
    From a cancer on the face, near Dallas, N. C., on the 25th
instant, Mrs. Mary Jenkins, consort of Aaron Jenkins, in the
80th year of her age.
    At Clay Hill, in this District, on the 11th instant, Maria
Albertine, daughter of John L. and M. M. Watson, aged twenty
three months....

Issue of September 6, 1860

    Married on the 29th of August, by James Jefferys, Magistrate,
Mr. Jonathan E. McLain, and Miss Lucy Ann Chambers, all of this
district.
    On Tuesday 28th of August, by Joseph Mccosh, Esq., Mr. William
McK. Mittag, of Lancaster Court House, S. C.,and Miss Mary Love
Wilson, daughter of Thomas Wilson, of Cleveland County, N. C.

Issue of September 13, 1860

    Married on Thursday morning, September 6th, by A. S. Wallace,
Esq.,Mr. Robert Nesbit of Ga.,and Miss Lizzie, daughter of Daniel
and Susan Peeler, of York District.
    Died in Gaston County, N. C., on the 7th inst., Calvin Thomp-
son, son of J. R. and S. S. Kincaid, formerly of Yorkville, aged
2 years and 6 months....
    At Rock Hill, York District, on Sunday morning, 9th instant,
Susan Alice, daughter of Dr. R. H. and J. S. Hope, aged 12 years,
1 month and nine days.
    At Johnstown, Bradley County, Arkansas, on the 24th ult.,
Dr. Thomas Young Barron, aged 26 years and 18 days.
    In Yorkville, on Sunday 9th instant, Annie Gertrude, daughter
of George Steele, Esq., aged three years and six months.

Issue of September 20, 1860

    Married on Wednesday 12th instant, by Joseph McCosh, Esq.,
Mr. Henry Green and Miss Sarah C. Hill.
    On Wednesday evening, 12th instant, by Rev. W. W. Carothers,
Mr. R. W. Christian, of the "Rock Hill Chronicle," and Miss
Eliza A., daughter of Mr. John C. Wilson, all of this District.
    Died on Tuesday, the 11th instant, at her residence near
Bullock's Creek Church, in this district, and in the 26th year
of her age, Mrs. Mary Jane McNeel, wife of Mr. Gustavus L. McNeel...
leaves a husband and three children...(eulogy)

Issue of September 27, 1860

    Married on the 18th instant, by William McGill, Esq., Mr. Hugh
R. Wallace and Miss Martha L. Venable, all of this District.
    In Lincoln county, N. C., on Thursday, 18th instant, by Rev.
A. J. Fox, Mr. John A. Killian and Miss Carrie Rudisel, all of
Lincoln County, N. C.
    Died in this district, on the 19th instant, Louesia Ann,
daughter of H. B. and Mary A. Wallace, aged seven years and six
months...

Near Bethel, on the 17th instant, Zerraviah Helen Caroline,
daughter of Joseph and Sarah Brandon, aged 6 years.
In this district, on the 24th instant, Sarah E., daughter of
Jno and Mary Ferguson, aged 4 years.
In Gaston County, N. C., on Sunday, 23d instant, J. McElwee,
second son of Rev. E. E. and R. E. Boyce, aged 3 years and 3
months.

Issue of October 4, 1860

Married on Thursday evening, 20th instant, by Rev. W. W. Caro-
thers, Mr. Jno. R. Hogue, and Miss Elizabeth M., daughter of Capt.
Saml Smith, all of this district.
Died in this district on the 23d ultimo, Mrs. Nancy L. Mit-
chell, wife of Mr. Dawson Mitchell, aged 44 years.
In this district on the 26th ult., William Leslie, son of G.
L. and Mary Jane McNeel, aged 2 years, 9 months and 12 days.
In Gaston county, N. C., on Friday, 28th ultimo, Gardiner
Spring, eldest son of Rev. E. E. and R. E. Boyce, aged 5 years.

Issue of October 11, 1860

Married on Tuesday 2nd instant, by Rev. R. Y. Russel, Mr.
James M. Henry of Arkansas, and Miss Marsaline M. Black of York
District.
On Thursday, 4th instant, by Rev. R. Y. Russel, Mr. John H.
Hood and Miss Eliza C. Feemster, all of this District.
On Thursday, 4th instant, by Rev. R. Y. Russel, Dr. Minor
Gwin, of this District, and Miss Jane M. Ross, of Chester District.
Died in Gaston County, N. C., on the 21st ult., Wyatt M.
Gladden, aged 27 years, 8 months and 16 days....

Issue of October 25, 1860

Married at the residence of Mr. James Robinson, by Rev. E. A.
Price, on the 11th instant, Mr. W. A. Barber, of York District,
and Miss Mary R. Wright, formerly of Chester District.
On Thursday, 11th instant, by D. K. Bates, Esq., Mr. Wm.
Rawls, and Miss Ann Dickey, all of this District.
Died in Yorkville on the 11th instant, Robert Crenshaw,
youngest son of Joseph A. McLean, aged on year and two months.
In Union District, on the 18th instant, Miss Carrie M. Farr,
only daughter of H. G. & M. L. Farr.

Issue of November 1, 1860

Died on the morning of the 28th ultimo, Andrew Blum, infant
son of Asbury and Eliza C. Coward....
In this District on the 10th ultimo, John James, son of John
and Elizabeth White, aged 2 years, 5 months and 15 days.
IN this District, on the 29th ultimo, Luticia Jane, daughter
of Matthew and Catharine White, aged 3 years 2 months and 14 days.
In Yorkville, on Sunday, 28th ultimo, Mrs. Nancy Blair, in the
85th year of her age.
Died at his residence in Mecklenburg County, N. C., on the
15th of October, Mr. Andrew Springs, in the 75th year of his age...
member of the Presbyterian Church (long eulogy).

Issue of November 8, 1860

Married in Yorkville on Wednesday evening, 31st ult., by Rev. W. W. Ratchford, Mr. J. M. Partlow, and Mrs. Catharine Bridges, all of Yorkville.

In Yorkville, on Wednesday morning, 7th instant, by James Jefferys, Esq., Mr. Thomas Jackson Beard, of Gaston co., N. C., and Miss Emily L. Massey, of the former place.

Died on the 29th ult., of Typhoid Fever, Mr. James W. Fewell, in the 27th year of his age.

On the 2nd inst., of Typhoid Fever, Mrs. Jane, wife of James W. Fewell, in the26th year of her age....left an infant daughter.

Issue of November 15, 1860

Died in this place on Saturday night, Oct. 27th, Mrs. Nancy Blair, having a few days before closed her 84th year...widow of John Blair, Esq, who died 12 years since...a native of Ireland, daughter of Mr. John Erwin, came to America when she was about 12 years of age, and settled in Iredell County, N. C., a few miles north of Statesville...(long account and eulogy)

Died in this District on Sunday, 11th November, Mrs. Sarah Rooker, in the 66th year of her age.

In this District on Wednesday, 7th instant, Mr. James A. Barnett, in the 60th year of his age.

In this District on the morning of the 9th instant, near Bethel, Mrs. Mary Clinton, in the 82nd year of her age.

In this District at the residence of his father, on the 10th instant, Mr. Wm. B. Russell, a young man of much amiability and promise.

Issue of November 22, 1860

Married in Yorkville on Thursday evening the 15th instant, by Rev. L. A. Johnson, Mr. William L. Grist, and Miss Mary Frances Kerr.

Died in this District on the 10th inst., Mr. William B. Russell, in the 36th year of his age...born in Union District, S. C., 9th of July 1825...(long account and eulogy).

On Saturday 17th instant, Miss Mary Patrick, aged about 65 years.

On the 18th instant, Mrs. Sarah Ward, in the 31st year of her age, leaving a husband and four children...member of the M. E. Church....

Issue of November 29, 1860

Married in Unionville, on the 3d instant, by Rev. Mr. Seymour, Mr. Samuel Rainey Jr., of Yorkville, and Miss Julia B. Simms, of the former place.

On the 27th instant, by Rev. J. A. Davies, Mr. James McNinch, of Chester, and Miss Eliza Jackson, of York District.

Died August 29th, in the 37th year of her age, Mrs. Mary m., wife of Capt. A. G. Neel, Steel Creek, N. C...deceased was nurtured in the Presbyterian Church....

Issue of December 6, 1860

Married on the evening of the 27th ultimo, by Rev. J. M. H. Adams, Mr. James Mason and Miss Mary S., daughter of Mrs. Cynthia

Moore, all of Yorkville.

On the 22nd ultimo, by S. G. Brown, Esq., Mr. Elijah Mc-
Swain and Miss Harriet C. Jackson, all of this district.

On the 22nd ult., by A. Hardin, Esq., Mr. James Newton Peeler,
of Union District, and Miss Lavina Catharine Hambright, of York
District.

At "Rose's Hotel," in Yorkville, on Monday, 3d instant, by
Saml. W. Melton, Esq., Mr. O. W. Torrence, and Mrs. Nancy Morris,
formerly of Chester District.

Died at Pineville, N. C., on the 21st ultimo, Dr. Geo. W.
Campbell, in the 34th year of his age. He was a successful prac-
titioner of Medicine...member of the Presbyterian Church.

Issue of December 13, 1860

Married on Tuesday 11th instant, by A. S. Wallace, Esq., Mr.
Chelsea McCalla, of Tunnel Hill, Georgia, and Miss Frances A.,
daughter of William E. and Sarah Gunn, of York District, S. C.

On the 6th inst., by Rev. Robt. Lathan, Mr. Gilbert Aikin and
Miss Mary Adkin, all of York District.

Died at his residence at Louisiana, Pike Co., Missouri, on
Saturday, the 18th of June, Mr. Joseph Carroll, in the 79th year
of his age..born in York District, S. C., 25tł of September 1781.
At the age of 29 was married to Miss Isabella Henry. He joined
the Seceder Church in 1812...In 1817, he moved with his wife and
four children to Pike County, Missour, and settled on a farm on
Buffalo Creek....

Issue of December 20, 1860

Died in this district, on the 4th instant, Mr. John Swann,
in the 72d year of his age....member of Bethesda Presbyterian
Church....

Issue of January 3, 1861

Married in Yorkville, on the 27th ultimo, by Rev. R. Y. Russell, Mr. William McD. Palmer, of Spartanburg, S. C., and Miss
Sallie J. Tomlinson, of ths former place.

In York Sitrict, on the 13th ultimo, at the residence of the
bride's father, Dr. W. Harper Thomasson (Editor of the Rock Hill
Chronicle), to Miss L. L. Steele.

On the 19th ultimo, by Rev. L. A. Johnston, Mr. J. Wilson
Marshall, of Colleton District, and Miss Mary Ann, eldest daughter
of Wm. I. and Martha Clawson, of Yorkville.

On the 16th ultimo, by A. Hardin, Esq., Mr. John L. Doggett,
of Rutherford County, N. C., and Miss Margaret Rebecca Wood, of
York District.

On the 5th ultimo, by James Atkinson, Esq., Mr. John Meek
and Miss Nancy A. Sanders.

On the 18th ultimo, Mr. T. M. Gwinn and Miss Sarah S. S.,
daughter of Mr. E. and Sarah Sanders.

In Charlotte, on the 24th ultimo, by Rev. F. A. Mood, Mr.
W. J. Sprinkle, and Miss Mary S. Holton, second daughter of T. J.
Holton, of the North Carolina Whig, all of Charlotte, N. C.

On the 27th ultimo, by Rev. John S. Harris, Mr. James M. Poag
and Miss Clarissa C., daughter of Samuel Beamguard, Esq., all of
this district.

Near Shelby, N. C., on the 27th ultimo, by Rev. Mr. Holmes,
Mr. D. F. Jackson of York District, and Miss P. H. Elliott, of
the former place.

Issue of January 10, 1861

Married in Yorkville, on Sunday 6th instant, by Rev. W. C. Patterson, Mr. William A. Jeffreys, and Mrs. Dicey Horney, all of this place.

At the First Presbyterian Church, in Charleston on the 26th ultimo, by Rev. John Forrest, D. D., Mr. J. Forrest Gowan ("Willie Lighthear"), and Mary Carrie, daughter of the late Samuel Linley, Esq., all of Charleston, S. C.

Issue of January 24, 1861

Married in Shelby County, Alabama, on Tuesday, January 8th, by Rev. Mr. Roach, Mr. Richmond D. Looney, of the former place, and Miss Mattie J., daughter of Mr. Matthew and Mrs. M. B. Harper, formerly of Yorkville.

Issue of January 31, 1861

Married at Columbia, Maury county, Tennessee, on Thursday, 28th of December 1860, Mr. Wm. Saunders of that place, and Miss Alice Knowles, daughter of C. B. Knowles, formerly of Yorkville.

Died of chronic affection in this District, on the 22d, Rachel Nancy Rebecca, daughter of Caleb and Nancy Ann Gassaway, in the 30th year of her age.

Issue of February 7, 1861

Married at the residence of the bride's father, on the 31st ultimo, by Rev. p. M. H. Adams, Mr. William C. Gist, of Union, and Miss Fannie D. Crenshaw, of this place.

Issue of February 14, 1861

Died in Gaston county, North Carolina, on the 28th of January, Mr. J. R. Stowe, aged 51 years.

Issue of February 28, 1861

Death of William M. Martin, of the Enquirer.

Married in York District, on Tuesday, 12th instant, by J. D. P. Currence, Mr. J. A. Cathey and Mrs. Isabella Underwood, both of Mecklenburg Co., N. C.

Died on the 10th instant, Mary Ida, daughter of B. J. and M. L. Adams, aged 1 years, 11 months and 6 days....

Issue of March 7, 1861

Married in Gaston county, k. C., on the 27th ultimo, by Rev. E. E. Boyce, Mr. William A. Pearson, and Miss Nancy E. Weir.

Issue of March 14, 1861

Married on the 7th inst., by Rev. S. L. Watson, Mr. S. M. Fewell and Miss R. E. Barnett, all of this district.

Issue of March 21, 1861

Married on Tuesday 12th instant, by Rev. R. Y. Russell, Rev. James S. Bailey of Chester District, and Miss Elvira C. Gill, of york District.

On Tuesday, 12th instant, by Rev. Robt. Y. Russell, Mr. Thomas Burris and Miss Martha Williams, all of York District.

On Wednesday evening 13th instant, by Rev. James M. H. Adams, M. I. Donom Witherspoon, and Miss Margaret E. Wright, all of Yorkville.

In Yorkville, on the 14th instant, by John G. Enloe, Esq., Mr. William H. Howell, of Mississippi, and Miss Caroline Chambers, of York District.

Died at her residence in this District on the 6th inst., Mrs. Margaret A. Smarr, wife of Mr. J. D. Smarr, in the 30th year of her age...left a husband and two small children....(eulogy)

Issue of March 28, 1861

Married on Thursday 21st instant, by Rev. Samuel L. Watson, Mr. G. M. A. C. Riddle and Miss Mary M. Glenn, all of this District.

Dr. Andrew Jackson Berry was born in York District, January 4th, 1833 and died at his father's residence, March 25th, 1861... member of the M. E. Church....   J. W. North

Issue of April 4, 1861

Died in this District on the 9th ultimo, William Jefferson, infant son of Hugh B. and Margaret C. Hemphill, aged 1 year, 2 months and 12 days.

Issue of April 11, 1861

Married in Pine Bluff, Arkansas, on Tuesday, 19th ultimo, by Rev. J. A. Stanely, Col. Jos. H. Black, of Little Rock, to Miss Lizzie M., daughter of Gen. James Yell.

On the 4th instant, by Rev. J. A. Davies, Capt. Robert A. Caldwell, of York District and Miss Catherine J. Adams, of Gaston County, N. C.

Issue of April 18, 1861

Died in Gaston county, N. C., on the 12th instant, Isabella Higgins, in the 18th year of her age.

At the residence of Dr. C. P. Sandifer, on the 25th of November, Robert C. Barry, aged 14 years. He leaves one sister....

Married at Hood's Factory, by J. P. Hood, Esq., on Tuesday, 2d instant, Mr. John Colvin, of Chester District, and Mrs. Francis Narcissa Morgan, of York.

Issue of April 25, 1861

Died in this District on the 14th instant, and in the 23d year of his age, Wm. Thomas Hanna...his grandfather and father being elders in Bethesda Church....(eulogy)...a volunteer in the ranks of the Whyte Guards....

Issue of May 2, 1861

Married on the 18th ultimo, by J. D. P. Currence, Esq., Mr. Rufus Dobson and Miss Harriett A. Hemphill, all of York District.

(Beginning with the issue of May 7, this paper becomes a semi-weekly, bieng published on Tuesday and Friday).

Issue of May 10, 1861

Married on Thursday the 2nd instant, by Rev. W. W. Carothers, Mr. J. A. Smith and Miss Mary Jane, eldest daugher of Mr. J. A. Hogue, all of this district.
Died at his residence near Bullocks Creek Church, in this District, Mr. Arthur Kirkpatrick, in the 70th year of his age... member of the Presbyterian Church, and a ruling Elder for the last 25 years....

Issue of May 14, 1861

Account of the hanging at Shelby, N. C., of Martin Scruggs of Cleveland County.
Died on the 7th inst., Sarah Z., infant daughter of Mr. J. M. and Mrs. Elizabeth M. Cain, aged 9 months and 17 days....

Issue of May 17, 1861

Married on the 7th instant, by Rev. J. W. North, Mr. Natty B. Morgan, of Murfreesboro', Tenn., and Miss Cynthia E. Smith, of York District.
Died in this District on the 10th instant, Miss Abigail R. Anders, in the 42nd year of her age.

Issue of May 21, 1861

Died in Yorkville, on Saturday, 18th instant, Bessie Laird, youngest daughter of J. C. and M. E. Miller, ged 11 months and 30 days.
Suddenly, in this District on the 9th instant, Mr. Gilbert Enloe, in the 86th year of his age.

(Beginning with the issue of May 30, 1861, the paper resumes its weekly status).

Issue of May 30, 1861

Died in Mecklenburg County, N. C., on the 22d instant, Dr. W. A. Ardrey, formerly of York District, aged 63 years.

Issue of June 6, 1861

Tribute of Respect to the death of Mr. G. W. Mason, a member of the Catawba Light Infantry, at Bethel Church....left wife and children.

Issue of June 13, 1861

Died in Yorkville, on Saturday the 8th inst., William E., infant son of John R. and Mary J. Alexander, aged fourteen months.

Issue of June 20, 1861

Died in this District on the 19th instant, Charles B. Steele, at the age of about 25 years....(eulogy).

Issue of June 27, 1861

Died on the 15th instant, at the residence of her mother, Mrs. Sarah Sadler, in this District, Mrs. Elizabeth M. Moore, in the 32nd year of her age...left a husband and two little children. (eulogy).

Issue of July 4, 1861

Married in Gaston County, N. C., on the 20th ultimo, by D. F. Ragan, Esq., Mr. John H. Moore and Miss F. Cal. Glenn, all of Gaston.

Died in Yorkville, on Monday, 1st instant, Mrs. Martha L. Whitesides, wife of J. M. Whitesides and daughter of M. Mullino, aged about 25 years.

At Pleasant Ridge, Gaston County, N. C., on the 26th of June, John Franklin, son of David A. and Lodema Jenkins, aged on year, one month and 23 days.

On Sullivan's Island, on the 25th ult., James Addison, infant son of Capt. John L. and Mary P. Black, aged one year and eight months.

In this District, on the 23d ultimo, Wm. Hall, son of J. F. and M. A. Carothers, aged about two years.

In this District on the 20th ultimo, Mrs. C. Louisa Garrison, at the age of about 35 years...wife of P. Garrison, a Ruling Elder in Ebenezer Church....

Issue of July 11, 1861

Married on the 29th ultimo, by A. Hardin, Esq., Mr. John Starnes, of Cleveland County, N. C., and Miss Mary M. Manning, of York District, S. C.

Issue of July 18, 1861

Married on the 4th instant, by A. Hardin, Esq., Mr. George W. Moore, and Miss E. Jane Wylie, all of this District.

On Tuesday evening, the 16th instant, by Rev. W. W. Carothers, Mr. Joseph H. Mendenhall, of Sebastian County, Ark., and Mrs. Esther L. O'Daniel, of Gaston County, N. C.

Died in this District on the 13th instant, Miss Polly Floyd, in the 83d year of her age.

Issue of August 1, 1861

Death of Lieut. Richard A. Palmer, who fell in the terrible conflict at Stone Bridge, on the 21st july...born in Yorkville, S. C. 3 Sept 1833, graduated at the Citadel Academy in Charleston. (eulogy).

Died in camp, near Anquia Creek, Va., on the 15th of July, Wm. M. McGill, formerly of York District, and late a member of the "Monticello Guards," of Drew County, Arkansas.

Issue of August 15, 1861

Died of measles at Charlottesville, Va., on the 4th inst.,
Mr. M. F. Howell, Company A., of the 5th Regt., S. C. V. Mr.
Howell was of Union district, and son of Mrs. Mary Howell.

Issue of August 22, 1861

Died on the 11th instant, at the residence of her son, J. P.
Hood, Mrs. Mary Hood, aged about 88 years.
In this District on the 17th instant, W. F. Smith, son of
Calvin D. Smith, aged 20 years and 9 months.

Issue of August 29, 1861

Married on the 20th instant, by Rev. Lewis McSwain, Blanton
Moore, Esq., and Miss Sallie E. Goforth, all of this District.
Died in Virginia, on the 20th instant, Mr. James H. Cath-
cart, aged 24 years, 11 months and 24 days....(eulogy)

Issue of September 5, 1861

Died in this District on the 25th instant, Mrs. Mary Good, in
the 23d year of her age...leaves a husband and two little daughters....

Issue of September 19, 1861

Died in Rusk County, Texas, on the 18th ultimo, Mr. James M.
Patrick, formerly of York District, aged 67 years.

Issue of September 26, 1861

Married on Wednesday, the 18th instant, by Rev. J. M. H. Adams,
Capt. R. Leander Tomlinson, and Miss Martha S. Wright, all of
this District.
Died of Typhoid Fever, at the camp near Germantown, in Virginia,
on the 17th instant, William A. Youngblood, son of Samuel C.
and Lucy Youngblood, in the 21st year of his age. (eulogy)...
remains were brought home and buried in the churchyard at Bullock's
Creek....
Mr. P. P. Darwin was born in York Dist., May 29, 1840 and
died in Richmond, Va., at the residence of Mr. John D. Smith,
September 2, 1861...member of the Jasper Light Infantry...member
of the M. E. Church....

Issue of October 3, 1861

Married in Yorkville on the 1st instant, by Rev. J. S. Harris,
Mr. T. Simpson Tipping, and Miss Esther E., daughter of Dudley
Jones, Esq.
In Yorkville on the 1st instant, by John G. Enloe, Esq., Mr.
Thos. J. Neely, and Miss Tabitha A. Adkins.

Issue of October 10, 1861

Died in this place on Monday morning last, Mr. W. Calvin Purseley, aged about 19 years...Palmer Guards, Capt. McCorkle's Company.
In this District, on the 15th ultimo, Mrs. Rachel Warren, aged
83 years and ten months.

Issue of October 24, 1861

Married in this District on the 10th instant, by J. G. Enloe, Esq., Mr. Alexander Wallace and Miss Catharine Harvey, all of this district.
On the 11th inst., by J. G. Enloe, Esq., Mr. Allison Mitchell and Miss Martha Jane Mitchell, all of this District.
Died in this town, September 21st, Mr. F. H. Simril...(eulogy)

Issue of October 31, 1861

Died at the residence of S. C. Youngblood, Esq., in this District, the 22nd inst., Mr. Thomas Nancy, in the 56th year of his age...member of Capt. White's Company, from York, attached to the 4th Regt, S. C. V....(eulogy)
In this District on the 26th inst., Mr. John Fitchett, in the 68th year of his age....
On the 19th instant, at the residence of Mary Wllace, in Gaston County, N. C., Mrs. Charlotte Williams, in the 73d year of her age.

Issue of November 7, 1861

Married on Thursday last, by Rev. J. R. Baird, Mr. Elijah Warren and Miss Sarah Ann Henderson, all of York District.
On Monday evening, 4th instant, by John G. Enloe, Esq., Mr. Franklin Gardner and Miss Elizabeth Clark, all of this District.
Died in the hospital near Columbia, Sept. 25th, private Nicholas Calvin Goudelock, in the 29th year...member of Capt. McCorkle's co. from York, but a native and citizen of Union District...leaves five fatherless and motherless sisters....

Issue of November 28, 1861

Married on the 12th instant, by Rev. John S. Laird, Mr. Robert J. Smith, of York District, S. C., and Miss Sarah Kelly, of Tippah County, Miss.
On Wednesday, the 20th instant, by J. D. Wylie, Esq., Mr. Alexander Ramsey, of Cleveland, N. C., and Miss Martha Jane Wallace, of this District.
Died at the residence of Mrs. Wright in this District, on Friday, the 22nd inst., Mrs. A. Fannie Melton, wife of Mr. George W. Melton, in the 25th year of her age...(long eulogy).

Issue of December 5, 1861

Died in this District on the 24th ultimo, Mrs. Hannah Currence, in the 79th year of her age.
In this District, on the 25th ultimo, Mr. E. M. Jackson, in the 67th year of his age...left a large family and many friends....
In this place, on Sunday last, Mrs. Ann D. Galbraith, in the 69th year of her age.

Issue of December 12, 1861

Died at his residence in Yorkville, on Sabbath evening, 1st inst., Dr. William Moore, in the 71st year of his age...a native of York District...(long account and eulogy).
At Rock Hill, York District, on Sunday, the 1st inst., Mr. John C. Aycock, aged 40 years.

Issue of December 19, 1861

Died at the Hospital, in Richmond, Va., on the 9th inst., Mr. Robert P., son of Hugh and Elizbaeth A. Venable, in the 21st year of his age...a member of the King's Mountain Guards, 5th Regt., S. C. V....

Issue of January 2, 1862

Died of a complicated disease, at the residence of his father in Cleveland County, N. C., on the 14th ultimo, James A. Borders, in the 22d year of his age....(eulogy and account).

Issue of January 9, 1862

Died on the 20th of December last, on the bloody field of Drainesville, Va., 1st Lieut. Frederick E. Moore, in the 26th year of his age...youngest son of the late Dr. William Moore of Yorkville....

Issue of January 16, 1862

Married on the 7th instant, by Wm. McGill, Esq., in the house of the bride's father, Mr. Samuel McCarter, and Miss Mary A. Niell, all of this District.

Died at Little Rock, Arkansas, on the 8th day of October last, Rev. A. Williams, in the seventy-second year of his age, a native of York District.

At his residence in Union District, S. C., on the 3d of December last, Col. Nathaniel Gist, in the 86th year of his age.

In this District on the 11th instant, Mrs. Elizabeth F. McCarter, aged 76 years.

Issue of January 23, 1862

Died in Yorkville, S. C., on the morning of January 16th, 1862, Mr. Pinckney Wilson, son of Mr. George Wilson of York District...born May 11th, 1845....17th Regt., S. C. V.

In this District on the 16th inst., Charlton Wilson, infant son of Mr. J. C. and Mrs. F. J. McCarter, aged 4 months.

IN this district, on the 13th inst., Mr. George Turner, in the 72d year of his age.

Issue of January 30, 1862

Married on the 19th ultimo, in Tuscaloosa County, Alabama, at the residence of David Elliott, Esq., by Rev. T. S. Winn, Mr. John J. Mills, formerly of York District, and Miss Mary E. Elliott, of the former place.

On Tuesday last, by the Rev. R. A. Ross, Mr. E. H. Davis, of N. C., and Miss Margaret A., second daughter of Mr. J. L. Sutton, of York District.

Died at Camp Lee, near Charleston, on the 12th of January, J. G. Mullinax, of York District on the 31st year of his age... Capt. Wilson's Co., 17th Regt., S. C. V...

In this District, on the 21st inst., Mrs. Elizabeth C., wife of Joel McCarter, aged 47 years.

Issue of February 6, 1862

Married on Thursday the 30th of January, by J. D. Wylie, Esq., Mr. T. L. Whitesides of York District, and Miss Margaret Brown, of Union District.

Issue of February 13, 1862

Died in this District, on the 2nd inst., Mrs. Margaret Mc-Ilwain, in the 76th year of her age.

Issue of February 20, 1862

Died on the morning of the 14th instant, at Raleigh, N. C., Samuel H. P. Barron of Yorkville, S. C., aged 19 years and one month...member of the Jasper Light Infantry, (Capt. Seabrook), 5th Regt. S. C. V. (Col. Jenkins)...(account and eulogy).

Issue of February 27, 1862

Married on the 12th inst., by J. D. Wylie, Esq., Mr. Washington Childers and Miss Sarah J. Ramsey, all of York District.

Died at Centreville, February 16, 1862, John E. Love...(eulogy)

Issue of March 6, 1862

Died in the hospital at Charleston, on the 19th of January, 1862, Mr. R. Leander Tomlinson...18th Regt., S. C. V., Gadberry. (eulogy)

In Gaston County, N. C., on the 25th ultimo, Mrs. Margaret R., wife of W. M. Nolen.

Of Croup, at the residence of Mr. Walter Quinn, Etta and Carrie, aged respectively 1 years, 11 months and 19 days; and 11 months and 4 days, daughters of J. E. Quinn.

Issue of March 13, 1862

Married on the 4th instant, by Rev. John S. Harris, Mr. William Y. Jones and Miss Margaret E., daughter of John C. Tipping, all of York District.

On Monday evening, 10th inst., by Rev. Richard Furman, D. D., Corp. William W. East, of Yorkville, S. C., and Miss Sarah E., daughter of Mr. N. E. and Mrs. E. Whitmire, of Greenville, S. C.

Died in this District on the 5th inst., at the residence of her mother, Mrs. Martha J. Smith, consort of Z. D. Smith, and daughter of William and Eliza Glenn, aged 34 years...left seven children, the youngest 5 weeks old, and a husband....

In this District, on the 10th inst., Nannie J., youngest daughter of Mr. Leander Dobson, aged 4 years, 11 months and 10 days.

Issue of March 20, 1862

Died in this District on the 16th instant, Charlie, youngest son of Wm. Thomason, aged about two years.

Issue of March 27, 1862

Married on Sunday morning, 23d instant, by Rev. W. S. Black, Mr. A. Garvin and Mrs. Sarah E. McClain, all of Yorkville, S. C.

Issue of April 3, 1862

Married on the 27th ultimo, by Rev. S. L. Watson, Col. R. N. Wilson, of Gaston County, N. C., and Miss Mary E. Adams, of this District.

Died inYorkville, on the 27th ultimo, Annie, youngest daughter of Alfred and Cornelia Craven, aged one year, 2 months and 27 days....

Departed this life on Sabbath, 30th March, in the 89th year of his age, McCaslan D. Wallace...came from Ireland to this country in the year 1773. During the voyage, Mrs. Wallace gave birth to a son, the subject of this obituary....

Issue of April 10, 1862

Died in this District on Tuesday, the 1st of April, Mrs. Elizabeth Floodin, aged about 69 years.

In this district, on the 29th ultimo, James, eldest son of Charles and Violet McIlwain, aged about 7 years.

Issue of April 17, 1862

Died in this District on Saturday, 12th instant, Mr. Alexander Pagan, aged about 80 years.

In this District on the 6th inst., Mrs. Jane Whitesides, consort of John Whitesides, aged about 67 years.

Issue of April 24, 1862

Died in this place on the 18th instant, Mrs. Rebecca L. Felts, formerly of South-Hampton County, Virginia, in the 62nd year of her age.

Issue of May 8, 1862

Married in this District on the 29th ultimo, by J. D. P. Currence, Esq., Mr. George F. Turner and Miss Emily D. McCarter, all of this District.

Issue of May 15, 1862

Died in Yorkville, on the 28th ultimo, Catharine Henrietta, youngest daughter of Dr. J. F. & R. G. Lindsay, aged 9 years and 7 months.

Died in Richmond, Va., Mr. John J. Simril, son of H. H. and Nancy Simril, in the 22nd year of his age...a native of York District, member of Catawba Light Infantry Co., 5th Regt., S. C. V. ...

Issue of May 22, 1862

Died in this District on the 1st inst., Samuel Fair, eldest son of Mr. S. L. and Mrs. R. M. Campbell, aged 4 years, 7 months and 17 days.

Fell--shot through the head, at the battle of Williamsburg, Va., on the 5th of May, 1862, in the 20th year of his age, Robert Love, only son of Saml G. Hemphill, Esq., of Guthriesville, S. C.

Issue of May 29, 1862

Died in this District on Sunday, 25th inst., John Franklin, third son of Wm. L. and Jane Brown, aged five years and one day.

At his residence in Canton, Miss., on the 3d inst., in the 86th year of his age, Benj. Chambers, Esq., formerly Ordinary of York District.

In this District on the 26th inst., Mr. Robert P. Jackson, son of Mr. Elias M. Jackson, in the 36th year of his age.

Issue of June 5, 1862

Died in this District on the 26th ult., Mrs. Jane McCullough. in the 84th year of her age.

At her residence near Rock Hill, on the 26th ultimo, Mrs. Mary Isabella Mills, aged about 30 years.

Issue of June 19, 1862

Died at camp Pillow, Johns Island, on the 12th May, Mr. Samuel W. Beamguard, in the 26th year of his age...Carolina Rifles, 17th Regt. S. C. V.

At Camp Winder, in Richmond, Va., on the 3rd inst., Private Archibald W. Strain, of Co. A., 19th Regt. S. C. V., aged 18 years and 7 months.

In this District on the 15th inst., Miss Polly Miller, aged about 70 years.

Issue of June 26, 1862

Died in Yorkville, on the 17th inst., Sallie Lorenna, daughter of Rev. L. M. Anderson, aged 6 years and 20 days....

In Yorkville, on the 29th inst., in the camp...Edward M. Murphy, printer, aged 21 years and four months...Palmer Guards, 19th Regt., S. C. V....

Issue of July 10, 1862

Death of William W. East, principal editor of this paper, at the residence of his father in Laurens District, on the 29th ult., aged about 25 years...graduate of Erskine College, Abbeville District....

Died in this District on Friday, the 4th inst., Dr. W. J. Good, aged about 40 years.

On the 7th inst., Mary Elizabeth, eldest child of James W. and Elizabeth Fewel, aged 6 years and 11 months....

Issue of July 17, 1862

Wm. W. East, son of William and Bethiah East, died at his father's residence in Laurens District, on the 29th June, from a wound received a Seven Pines....(eulogy)

In this District on the 13th inst., Mr. J. Brison Venable, aged 49 years.

Issue of July 24, 1862

Died in Shelby County, Alabama, on the 23d of June, Mrs. Mary Alexander, aged about 80 years, relict of Mr. Henry Alexander, deceased, formerly of York District.

At his residence near McConnellsville, S. C., on the 5th inst., Mr. Philander Moore, in the 82nd year of his age...member of Bethesda Church for 60 years....

In this District, on the 7th inst., and in the 42nd year of her age, Mrs. Margaret, wife of Mr. Charles Curry...left an aged mother, a husband, and six little children...

July 10th, on his way home, in York District, from a wound received in one of the late battles before Richmond, Va., Cpl. Jno. W. Lindsay, in the 30th year of his age...McCorkle's Co., 12th Regt. S. C. V....

Issue of July 31, 1862

Married on Tuesday the 22nd inst., by Rev. Mr. Brearley, Capt. John A. Witherspoon, Company C., 17th Regt., S. C. V., to Miss Bettie E., daughter of the late Wm. E. James, of Darlington Dist., S. C.

On the 29th instant, by Rev. S. L. Watson, William A. Currence, and Miss Adeline Wallace, all of this District.

William Alexander Fewell, a native of York Dist., S. C., died at the Chesapeake Hospital, near Fort Monroe, Va., on the 24th of June, 1862, in the 16th year of his age....(verse)

AT Poplar Lawn Hospital, Richmond, Va., on the 8th inst., Sgt. William M. Brown, Co., B., 12th Regt., S. C. V., aged 30 years.

Issue of August 7, 1862

Died in the General Confederate Hospital, Richmond, Va., on the 7th July 1862, from a wound received on 1st July, Charles E. Moore, of Yorkville, S. C., aged about 28 years...leaves a wife and two small children....

Near this town, on the 29th ult., Mrs. Rachel Devinny, in the 41st year of her age. A few hours before she died, her infant was baptised....

Death of Corp. Jno. G. A. Holland, Co. I, 3rd Regt., S. C. V., near Richmond, June 29th, and died July 1st, aged 24 years....

Death of Corp. J. Wesley Boyd, who died July 2nd, aged 23 years...eldest son of Capt. Jas. and Mrs. Margaret Boyd, of Laurens District....

Issue of August 13, 1862

Died in Weldon, N. C., on the 17th ult., Friday, 27th of June, James Franklin Nesbit, in the 23rd year of his age...born in York District, S. C...(eulogy)

Near Richmond, Va.,on the 29th of June, William McDonald Palmer, aged 24 years, 1 month and 3 days...12th Regt. S. C. V....

In Yorkville, July 21, Minnie Caroline, 2d daughter of J. W. and L. S. Avery, aged 6 years....

Issue of August 20, 1862

Died at the South Carolina Hospital, Petersburg, Va., on the 10th inst., Thomas J. Boyd, of Co. H., 18th Regt., S. C. V., formerly of York District, aged about 22 years.

In this town, 9th inst., John Alfred, son of Mrs. Eliza A. Adams, aged 13 months....

Issue of August 27, 1862

Fell on the battle-field near Richmond, on the 30th of June last, Mr. John Rosborough, in the 28th year of his age...Capt. White's Co....

In this District on the 18th inst., Mr. David Byers, aged 87 years, 10 months and 13 days.

Issue of September 3, 1862

Died in this village, on the morning of the 31st ultimo, Edward Michael, second son of Thomas and Catharine O'Farrell, aged 16 years and 20 days....

Issue of September 10, 1862

Died in Yorkville on the 5th inst., Isaac Donnom, infant son of Capt. I. D. and Mrs. M. E. Witherspoon, aged 6 months and 19 days....

Died on the 24th ult., of Camp Fever, in the Chisholm Hotel, at Hanover C. H., Va., 1st Lieut. J. Laban Grier, Co. B., 1st Regt., N. C. Cavalry...left a widowed mother.

Issue of September 17, 1862

Jonathan E. McClain of York District, was born 23d of March 1840, died on the battle-field of Manassas, on the 30th August 1862, aged 22 years and 5 months....left wife and infant child....

Issue of September 24, 1862

M. J. Hall, died at the private residence of Mrs. Blakenship, at Manchester, Va., on the 5th of June...son of A. Newton and Mrs. Nancy C. Hall, formerly of this District.

Oscar L. Wallace, a native of York Dist., born 31 Dec 1841 and killed at Manassas, Va., 30th August 1862, married young, and leaves a wife and child....

Issue of October 1, 1862

Died on the 27th of August, Thos. Campbell, son of Thomas C. and Clarissa Henry, aged 1 year, 10 months and 14 days.

On the 17th inst., James Leslie McElwee, in the 20th year of his age...connected himself with Catawba Light Infantry, 5th Regt., S. C. V....

Issue of October 8, 1862

Died in this District on the 27th ultimo, little Becca, daughter of J. E. & Mary Love, aged 3 years.

On the 28th ult., James E. Purseley, aged about 28 years. On the 30th ult., James Matthews, eldest son of A. J. Matthews, aged 12 years.

On the 1st inst., Mrs. Rebecca Jackson, wife of Capt. Wm. T. Jackson, aged 20 years...left a husband and two small children.

Issue of October 15, 1862

Died at Warrenton, Va., on the 14th Sept last, Lieut. J. H. Bigham, in his 26th year of wounds received at the battle of Manassas....

Issue of October 22, 1862

Death of Corp. John O. Montgomery, of Co. A., 12th Regt. S. C. V., killd. at the battle of Manassas, 20th August 1862, aged 20 years....

Issue of October 29, 1862

Died October 1st, at Warrenton, Va., of a wound received in the battle of Manassas, August 30th, Daniel Williams, son of Mr. J. J. Moore, of this District on the 21st year of his age....
At her residence in York District, on the 20th instant, Mrs. Mary Avery, wife of Edward Avery, Sr....
Death of James H. Kincaid, a native of York District, S. C., a member of Co. B., 12th Regt. S. C. V., killed 29 August 1862 at Manassas....

Issue of November 12, 1862

Died near Ebenezerville, York Dist., on the 4th Nov., Elizabeth Rebecca Jane, eldest daughter of J. T. & M. A. Matthews, aged ten years.

Issue of November 19, 1862

Married at the residence of Mrs. I. G. O'Neale, on Tuesday evening, 28th October, by James Aiken, Esq., Mr. Thomas D. Harris, of York District, a Corporal in the President Guards, Va. Volunteers, to Miss Susan E. Holly, daughter of the late John Holly, of Fairfield District, S. C.
At the house of the bride's father, on the 11th inst., by Rev. W. W. Carothers, Mr. S. W. Craig, of Gaston County, N. C., and Mrs. M. A. Martin, daughter of Mr. E. D. Thompson, of York District, S. C.
Died on the 2nd inst., Mary Louisa, youngest child and only daughter of D. D. Moore, in the 5th year of her age....

Issue of November 26, 1862

Died in this place on Sunday morning, last, Mary Helen, second daughter of Capt. L. M. and Mrs. Frances V. Grist, aged 4 years, 4 months and 2 days.
Died in Maryland, on the 19th of October, from a wound at Sharpsburg, R. Douglass Crawford, of this District, aged 29 years.
In this Town, on the 12th inst., Mrs. Margaret Amanda, wife of Captain Walter B. Metts, in the 32nd year of her age....
At his father's residence in York District, S. C.,on the 16th inst., James Edward Burns, in the 21st year of his age... Capt. McCorkle's Co., 12th Regt., S. C. V....

Issue of December 10, 1862

Died near this place on Wednesday evening, the 3d inst., John Robert, youngest son of J. J. and Margaret A. Snider, aged one year, eight months, and eight days.
Died at his residence in this district, on the 14th of Oct., 1862, Mr. James R. Clinton, in the 59th year of his age...member of the Independent Presbyterian Church, and a ruling elder....

Issue of January 14, 1863

Married on the 21st day of December last, by Joseph McCosh, Esq., Mr. Lawson Wilson and Miss Caroline Moore, all of York District.

In this District on the 6th inst., by John G. Enloe, Esq., Mr. Charles Curry and Miss Nannie L. Jones.

Died in Chester District, on the 2d of December last, Samuel Currence, eldest son of Mr. S. J. and Mrs. M. J. Hemphill, formerly of York District.

In this place on Friday, 9th inst., Mr. Matthew McCants, in the 55th year of his age.

In this place on Monday night, the 12th inst., Miss Hannah E. Alexander, daughter of the late Wm. R. Alexander, in the 25th year of her age.

Issue of January 21, 1863

Death of a Veteran Shipmaster. Died in this place on Monday, 19th inst., in the 76th year of his age, Capt. John Baker, formerly and for many years, Master of Packet Vessels running between Charleston and Philadelphia....

Died near Ebenezerville, on Tuesday, the 16th of December, 1862, little Lizzie, the only child of W. J. & M. S. Kimbrell, aged 2 years, 2 months and 2 days....

Issue of January 28, 1863

Died, near Bethel, in York District, S. C., on the 16th inst., Mrs. Eliza R. Adams, wife of J. L. M. Adams, and daughter of Robt. Robinson, deceased, of Chesterville...in the 36th year of his age....

Issue of February 11, 1863

Married on the 4th of February, instant, by Rev. J. W. Humbert, Mr. Wm. Dickson, and Miss Miriam Howell, all of York District.

Died in Gaston County, N. C., on the 1st inst., Mrs. Margaret M., wife of Capt. S. N. Stowe, in the 38th year of her age....

Issue of February 18, 1863

Died in this District on the 28th ultimo, Sylvanus Meek, youngest son of J. J. and N. J. Wylie, aged 8 months.

Issue of March 4, 1863

Died of erysipelas, in Gaston County, N. C., on the 23d of February, aged 2 years, 11 months and 12 days, Elizabeth Hoyle, daughter of Wm. I. and Jane C. Stowe....

Issue of March 18, 1863

Married at Waverly, near Columbia, on the 9th inst., by Rev. P. J. Shand, Brig. Gen. E. McIlver Law, of Alabama, and Jennie, daughter of William A. Latta, formerly of Yorkville.

Issue of April 1, 1863

Married on the 26th ultimo, by Rev. J. F. Watson, Mr. James McKeown, of York District, and Mrs. Margaret E. Whitesides, of Union District.

Died in Cleveland County, N. C., on the 2nd ultimo, Lieut. T. B. Hunt, of the 38th Regt. N. C. V.,in the 25th year of his age....

Departed this life at the residence of his son, Chas. E. Baker, in Yorkville, on January 19th, 1863, Capt. John Baker, in the 76th year of his age....

Issue of April 8, 1863

Died of consumption, at the residence of his father, at Blairsville, in this District, on Thursday morning, 2nd inst., E. Giles Russell, in the 29th year of his age...member of the Independent Presbyterian Church....

Issue of April 15, 1863

Married on the 31st ultimo, by Rev. S. L. Watson, Capt. Alexander Neel, of Mecklenburg County, N. C., and Miss A. M. C. Adams, of York District.

Issue of May 13, 1863

Married on Wednesday, the 6th of May, by the Rev. Mr. W. H. Hanckle, Brig. Gen. States Right Gist, Confederate States Army, to Miss Janie M., daughter of the late Ex-Governor James H. Adams, of South Carolina.

Died at his residence in Augusta, Georgia, on the 28th ultimo, Mr. Alexander H. Hemphill, a native of this District, in the 52nd year of his age.

Issue of May 27, 1863

Died near Yorkville, on the 18th inst., William B., son of Charles M. and Mary Pearson, in the eighth year of his age.

On the 18th inst., at his residence in this District, Mr. James Wallace, aged 68 years...for six years an elder in Bethel church....

At Ferdericksburg, on the 3rd inst., Lieut. J. M. T. Harper, Co. C., 49th Regt, Alabama Volunteers, formerly of York District.

Issue of June 3, 1863

Died in Gaston county, N. C., on the 20th ultimo, Mr. J. E. Strain, Co. E., 5th Regt., S. C. V., in the 29th year.

Issue of June 10, 1863

Died in Gaston County, N. C., on the 1st inst., Mr. S. F. D. Beird, aged 49 years.

On the 19th of April, near Franklin Station, Va., Mr. Lawson Clark, in the 36th year of his age.

Issue of June 17, 1863

Married in this District, at the residence of Mr. Walter Quinn, on the 3rd inst., by Rev. S. L. Watson, Mr. J.O. Moore, and Miss Drucilla B. Denham.

Issue of July 1, 1863

Death of Rev. R. W. Barnwell...in Virginia....
Married on the 18th June, at Hood's, in York District, by J. P. Hood, Esq., Mr. W. J. Robins, and Miss Mildred J. Barnes, of Chester District.

Issue of July 8, 1863

Died in this District on the 15th ultimo, Martha Desdemonah McElmoyl, only daughter of Sarah E. Moore, aged 13 years, one month and four days....

Issue of July 15, 1863

Married at the residence of the bride's father, on Wednesday, the 8th inst., by Rev. Mr. McCormick, Capt. I. N. Withers, C. S. A., of Yorkville, and Miss Mattie, daughter of James Caldwell, of Fairfield District.

Near Clinton, La., by Rev. W. F. Camp, Surgeon G. W. Broach of C. S. A., and Miss Lizzie Bryant, of Bossier Parish, La.

Died at the residence of his parents, in this Town, on the 6th inst., in Virginia, Foster G. Jefferys, youngest son of James and Elizabeth H. Jefferys, Co. G. Palmetto Sharpshooters, S. C. V., aged 19 years and 5 days....

Issue of July 22, 1863

Married in Fairfield District at the residence of the Bride's father, Col. G. H. Miller, on Saturday the 11th inst., by Rev. Mr. Erwin, Mr. William F. McFadden, of Yorkville, and Mrs. Sarah Young, of Fairfield District.

Issue of July 29, 1863

Married on Friday evening, 24th inst., by William McGill, Esq., Mr. Charles Simmons and Miss Dorcas, daughter of Lamuel Anders.

Issue of August 5, 1863

Death of Hon. W. L. Yancey, at his residence near Montgomery, Alabama...Senator from Alabama in the Confederate Congress....

Issue of August 26, 1863

Died near Highland, Ala., August 6th 1863, Hazel Smith, son of Matthew and Martha B. Harper, formerly of Yorkville, S. C... member of Co. G, 20th Regt., Alabama Volunteers....in the siege of Vicksburg.

Issue of September 2, 1863

Married on the 26th ultimo, by Rev. S. L. Watson, Mr. P. W. A. Neel of Mecklenburg County, N. C., and Miss C. M. Adams, of this district.

On Tuesday the 1st instant, by J. R. Wallace, Esq., Mr. John J. Adkins, and Miss Amanda, daughter of Wm. Boggs, all of York District.

Issue of September 9, 1863

Died in Yorkville, S. C., on the 30th ultimo, Jessie DuBois, youngest child of Colonel and Mrs. A. Coward, aged three months and thirteen days....

In Gaston County, N. C., on the 1st inst., Mrs. Mary J. Faires, in the 32nd year of her age....(eulogy).

Issue of September 16, 1863

Died in this District on the 30th ultimo, Joshua Walker, third son of Samuel W. and Rebecca T. Jackson, aged six years and nineteen days.

On the 3rd instant, James Jefferys, second son of Samuel W. and Rebecca T. Jackson, aged seven years, ten months and 12 days.

Issue of September 30, 1863

Married on the 22d instant, by Rev. J. R. Baird, Mr. G. W. Croat and Miss M. C. Wallace, all of this District.

Issue of October 7, 1863

Married on the 26th instant, by Rev. D. S. May, Mr. Wm. Felts and Emeline Jones, all of this District.

Died in this District on the 29th ultimo, Mrs. Margaret Chambers, in the 89th year of her age.

On Sunday, 27th September, of wounds received in the battle of Chickamauga, on the 20th, James Marion Meek, a member of Capt. A. T. Meek's Co, 2nd Regt, Arkansas Volunteers, Liddle's Bridage, Army of Tennessee....a native of this District, and for the late three years a resident of Arkansas.

Issue of October 21, 1863

Married on the 13th instant, by the Rev. John S. Harris, Mr. Bolivar Byers and Miss Mary C. Clark, all of this District.

Issue of October 28, 1863

Died in this District on the 5th inst., Miss Margret Hannah, daughter of John O. and Martha Jackson, in the 14th year of her age.

In this District on the 10th inst., Miss Violet Erixna Currence, in the 17th year of her age.

In this District on Saturday, the 24th inst., Mr. Arthur Parish, in the 67th year of his age.

Issue of November 18, 1863

Died on the 3rd inst., Myron Bratton, only son of Rev. John S. and Agnes B. Harris, aged about 3 years....

Of diphtheria, in this District, on the morning of the 4th inst., Battie Springs, daughter of Wm. S. and Margaret A. Moore, in the 10th year of her age....

Letter related the death of William Mitchell, son of Mr. John C. Mitchell....

Issue of November 25, 1863

Died in Yorkville, S. C., November 14th, 1863, Mr. Jerome C. Miller, aged 37 years and 2 days...a ruling elder in the Presbyterian Church in Yorkville....(long eulogy).

Issue of December 2, 1863

Death of Andrew Jackson Clanton, Co. K. 17th Regt. S. C. V., Nov. 26th, 1863. Two elder brothers had already fallen...A. J. Clanton was about 24 years of age....

Issue of December 9, 1863

Died in this District on the 30th ult., John B., son of William Bradford, in the 12th year of his age.

Col. Edward Avery Senr. departed this life on Nov. 24th, 1863 at his residence in Ebenezerville...a native of Va., but has been a resident of S. C. for near fifty years....

On the 29th Nov., Lula Wallace, only child of Oscar L. and M. C. Wallace, aged three years, one month and five days....

Issue of December 16, 1863

Died in Laurens District, December 1, 1863 , at the residence of her grandmother, Annie Toland, daughter of Walter B. Metts, Esq., of this place, in the 5th year of her age....

In Ebenezerville, Nov. 24th, Mr. Edward Avery, an aged and venerable citizen...born in Va., Nov. 11th, 1792, emigrated to S. C. in 1815....(eulogy)

Issue of December 23, 1863

Died in Yorkville on Monday morning,21st inst., Mrs. Jane Elizabeth, consort of Mr. Leander Garvin, in the 37th year of her age.

Married in this District on the 10th inst., by Rev. E. E. Boyce, Mr. J. J. Revels, of N. C., and Miss Mary Andres, of York District.

Issue of January 13, 1864

Married in this place on the evening of the 12th inst., at the brides residence by the Rev. E. G. Gage, Mr. H. Calvin Conner and Miss O'Leary, all of Yorkville.

Issue of January 27, 1864

Died at his fathers residence in York Dist., S. C.,on the 3d day of January ,1863, Austin S. Whitesides, son of Thos. White-

sides. This is the 2d and last son of his who has been sacrificed.
Austin S. Whitesides was born 2 April 1842. His brother James
H. Whitesides born 31 Aug 1832, Co. H. 1st S. C. Cavalry, and
died in Clayton Hospital, Lynchburg, Va., 20th March 1863.

Issue of February 3, 1864

Married on Thursday, 28th ultimo, by Rev. E. G. Gage, Mr.
George W. Jeffery and Miss Elizabeth C. Black, all of this District.
Died in this District on the 23rd ultimo, Mrs. Sarah Glass,
aged 85 years.

Issue of February 10, 1864

Died in this place on the 28th ultimo, James Edward, fourth
son of Col. R. G. & Mrs. B. M. McCaw, aged four years.

Issue of February 17, 1864

Died in this District on Thursday, the 11th inst., James M.
Faries, in the 16th year of his age.

Issue of March 9, 1864

Married on the 3d instant, by J. D. P. Currence, Esq., Mr.
John W. Parker, and Miss Seely ann Revel, all of Gaston County,
N. C.
Died in this District, on Sunday, the 28th of February, Mr.
Joseph Wallace, in the 87th year.
In Shelby, N. C., on the 22d ult., in the 14th year of her
age, Miss Sallie G. Mullineaux...funeral preached in the Baptist
Church.

Issue of March 16, 1864

Died in this District on the 7th inst., Mrs. M. C. Wallace,
in the 24th year of her age.

Issue of March 23, 1864

Died at his residence in York Dist., on the 12th inst., in
the 56th year of his age, Wm. Moore...a deacon of the Baptist
Church....

Issue of March 30, 1864

Married on the evening of the 22d inst., by Rev. R. Lathan,
Mr. E. P. Castles, of Fairfield District, and Miss Emma J.,
daughter of Jackson Brown, of this District.
Died on the 3rd of December last, William E. Murphy, a native
of York District, but for several years a citizen of Alabama...
was employed in the ENQUIRER OFFICE....about 30 years of age.

Issue of April 6, 1864

Married on the 31st ultimo, at the residence of the bride's
mother, by Rev. J. F. Watson, Mr. W. R. Moore, 1st S. C. C., and
Miss V. G., daughter of Mrs. Mary Jackson, all of this District.
Died in Yorkville, S. C., March 21, 1864, Mrs. Jane E. McLean,
daughter of Dr. E. A. Crenshaw, and wife of Col. Jos. A. McLean,

in the 30th year of her age....
On the 28th ult., Hugh McGinnis, a native of Ireland, but
for many years a resident of York Dist., aged about 70 years.
On the 23d ult., Mrs. Rachael Lathem, wife of J. G. Lathem,
aged about 27 years.

Issue of May 11, 1864

Death of Col. Jno. L. Miller...born in this District, he was
a son of Dr. John L. Miller (brother of Col. Stephen D. Miller,
Ex-Governor of this State)...graduated from Davidson College...
(long account).

Issue of May 18, 1864

Died in the hospital, at Florence, S. C., on the 6th inst.,
J. Meek Hope, in the 23d year of his age...buried in Smyrna
Churchyard...(long account)

Issue of June 1, 1864

Married on the 18th inst., by Rev. Wm. Crook, Mr. J. J. W.
Gassaway, and Miss Elizabeth Brewer, all of this District.

Issue of June 8, 1864

In Memoriam. Parks a Jackson, died at Clay's Farm, Chesterfield Co., Va., 20th May 1864....
George Hare Farrell was born in York District, 1st Nov 1841
and was wounded in the battle of the Wilderness, Va., 6 May 1864
from which he died....
Died in this place on Thursday, 2nd inst., of flux, James
Rufus, son of Mr. Thos B. and MaryAnn Jefferys, aged 3 years and
6 months.

Issue of June 15, 1864

Died in Abbeville Hospital, near Tennessee, on 16th May, James
A. Parish, a native of York Dist., Co. G. Palmetto Sharp Shooters,
aged 18 years and six months....
From a wound received in the Wilderness battle, near Chan-
cellorsville, Va., May 8, 1863, H. N. Owens, aged 24 years, 4
months and 3 days....
Lt. H. J. Costner, of 18th Regt., N. C. T., in the 25th year
of his age, killed 23d May 1864....

Issue of June 22, 1864

Sergt. Isaac N. Enloe, son of John G. Enloe, Esq., of Yorkville, killed on 20th ult., in the battle of Clay's Farm....aged
21 years....

Issue of June 29, 1864

Robert Love Devinny was born in York Dist., S. C., 5 May
1845, and was killed 20 May 1864, in the battle of Clay's Farm...
died in Hospital, 10th June....
Died, In Coosawhatchie, S. C., June 9, 1863, Pvt. John H.
Boyd, aged 37 years, 6 months and 7 days, leaving a wife and
five little children....

Issue of July 6, 1864

Married on Tuesday, 28th ult., by Rev. S. L. Watson, Capt.
H. D. Stowe, of Gaston, N. C., and Miss S. C. Tate, of York
District, S. C.
Died in this District on Monday, 27th ult., Mrs. Mary Sutton,
aged 83 years.
John J. Lamaster was born in York Dist., S. C., 9 april 1843,
and wounded 20th May 1864 at Clay's Farm, Va....

Issue of July 13, 1864

Died in Laurenceville, Ga., on the 29th ult., Robert Patrick
Spence, son of J. D. & F. B. Spence, aged 6 months and 4 days.
On Sunday, July 3rd, 1864, at the Fair Ground Hospital, Peters-
burg, Va., J. B. Brown, in the 23d year of his age....

Issue of July 27, 1864

Died on the 7th day of May, J. Albert Thomas, in the 33rd year
of his age, Co. A., 8th Regt. S. C. V....
At Brattonsville, on the 20th inst., Thomas Jefferson, son of
the late Maj. T. J. and Jane Dunovant....
Isaac Newton Sadler, son of Elijah and Ann Clark, of York
Dist., fell in his country's service, 23d May 1864...Co. A., 12th
Regt. S. C. V...church of Bethesda....
John O. Jackson, died at Winder Hospital, June 12th, 1864,
in the 41st year of his age...the last surviving member of the
family.
Died in this District, on the 18th inst., J. A. M. Aycock,
son of James P. and M. E. Aycock, aged 5 years, 5 months and 22
days.

Issue of August 3, 1864

Died at Field's Division Hospital, on the 16th of May, Pvt.
T. E. Burris...Co. E., 5th Regt., S. C. V....
On the 25th July 1864, at his home near Yorkville, S. C.,
J. J. R. Garvin, aged 18 years and 10 months...Co. F., 17th Regt.
S. C. V....

Issue of August 10, 1864

Died on the 20th of July, near Petersburg, Va., Mr. A. A. Bar-
ron, in the 28th year of his age.
On the 30th July, William C. Pollard, aged 18 years and 8 months.
Co. F., 17th Regt. S. C. V....
Killed at Petersburg, Va., on the 30th July,1864, Pvt. J.
Robt. Brown, Co. G. 18th Regt., S. C. V.

Issue of August 17, 1864

Lieut. S. C. Lowry, Co. F., 17th Regt., S. C. V., aged 19
years and 7 months killed 30th July....

Issue of August 24, 1864

Died on the 6th of May, R. C. Whitesides, Co. G. 12th Regt.,
S. C. V....
Of Measles, near Petersburg, June 15, 1864, James M. McGill.

Killed near Petersburg, 30th July 1864, Pvt. J. E. McCarter, Co.
G., 18th Regt. S. C. V....

Issue of August 31, 1864

Death of William S. Chambers, born 30 June 1842, killed 30th
July 1864 at Petersburg....

Issue of September 7, 1864

Died at the hospital in Petersburg, on the 7th of August,
William H. Hogue, in the 30th year of his age...born in York Dist.,
S. C., 2nd July 1834...deacon in the church.

Issue of September 14, 1864

Married on the 6th inst., by Rev. S. L. Watson, Mr. C. M.
Parrott, of 5th Regiment S. C. V., and Miss Mary G. Jackson, all
of this District.
In memory of Lt. R. A. Jackson, of Co. G., 18th Regt., S. C.
V., who was killed at Petersburg, Va., July 14th, 1864...leaves
a wife and one child.
On the 26th of August, in the 36th year of her age, Mrs.
Elizabeth, daughter of the late R. M. Love, and wife of Joseph
P. Moore, of McConnellsville....

Issue of September 21, 1864

Married on the 8th inst., at the residence of the bride's
father, at Ebenezerville, S. C., by Rev. L. McDonald, Mr. J. F.
Barron and Miss Jennie A. Killian.

Issue of October 5, 1864

Married on the 21st of September, by Rev. William Crook, Mr.
Thomas Wiley and Miss Bell Holmes, all of this District.
On the 26th September by John G. Enloe, Esq., Sergt. Samuel
L. Harvey of the 5th Regt., S. C. V., and Miss Elizabeth J. Jack-
son, all of this District.
Martha Wilkins was born Feb. 18, 1826,... joined the Baptist
Church in 1851; was married to Rufus Roberts, 24 May 1855, and
died September 18, 1864....left husband and four children....

Issue of October 26, 1864

The body of J. J. Coward was received here last evening from
Virginia, where he died...brother of Col. Asbury Coward, of the
5th Regt. S. C. V.

Issue of November 2, 1864

Married on the 25th October, by J. D. F. Currence, Esq., Dr.
Thomas W. Campbell and Miss Eliza Jane Staunton, all of York
District.

Issue of November 9, 1864

Died at his residence on the 23d of October, Mr. E. M. Henry,
son of Francis Henry, in the 50th year of his age....leaves a
wife and four children.

Davis McDonough Hope of Co. G., P. S. S. fell mortally wounded at Chaffins Farm, 30 Sept 1864, and died at Jackson Hospital
10 October, in his 25th year...buried by his brother Meek.

Issue of November 15, 1864

Married on the 7th instant, by William McGill, Esq., Corporal
James H. Yearwood, of the 5th S. C. V., and Miss Sarah Ann Horton,
all of this District.
Died at Gordonsville, Va., on the 29th of May, Sergeant
George Ross Burris, only child of John and Jane Burris, of York
District, S. C...left wife and two little sons...(eulogy).

Issue of November 23, 1864

Married on Wednesday morning, 19th instanty, by Rev. J. Monroe
Anderson, at the residence of the bride's father, Mr. A. K. Smith,
Co. A., 12th Regiment, S. C. V., and Miss Margaret S., daughter
of Mr. Samuel Steele, all of York District.

Issue of November 30, 1864

To the Memory of Arthur Crozier Ramsey, mortally wounded at
Piedmont, near Staunton, Va., June 5, 1864....(poem)

Issue of December 7, 1864

Died in the hospital, at Florence, S. C., on the night of the
26th November, James R., son of Robert and Minerva Turner, of
York District, aged 17 years and six months...Co., C., Reserve
Forces....   M. H. Currence, Chaplain.
John C. Brandon, Co. B., 5th Regt., S. C. V., died 16 Nov
1864...leaves father and mother, and sisters....

Issue of January 4, 1865

Married on the 13th ultimo, by Rev. J. A. Davies, Mr. Hugh
Nichols and Miss Emma F. Hudson, all of this District.
On the 20th ultimo, by Rev. J. A. Davies, Mr. W. R. Davies
and Miss Eliza A., daughter of S. G. Brown, Esq., all of this
District.
On the 9th of November last, by Templeton Black, Esq., Mr.
B. F. Little, 4th Texas Regiment, Longstreet's Corps, and Miss
Sue A. Owens.
In Memoriam. Rev. John S. Harris. Died at Brattonsville, York
District, Nov. 16, 1864, aged 32 years...a graduate of Davidson
College, N. C., in the class of 1856, enetered Theological Seminary
at Columbia...(long account and eulogy)...left widow and children.

Issue of January 18, 1865

Married on the 22d ult., by Rev. W. W. Carothers, at the
residence of Mrs. Simmons, Robert H. Craig, of Gaston County,
N. C., and Miss Nancy E. Hunter, of this District.

Issue of January 25, 1865

Married in Mississippi, on the 17th of November, by Rev. Mr.
Fox, Sergt. Thomas Bratton, and Miss A. C. Clarke, formerly of

Memphis, Tennessee.
Died at her residence in Chesterville, on the 3d of December, 1864, Mrs. Elizabeth Ellenor West, consort of E. J. West, Esq., aged 29 years, 3 months and 18 days....
In this District, on the 10th inst., George M., son of Robert and Manerva Turner...born Aug. 12th, 1841, Co. E., 17th Regt., S. C. V....
To the Memory of H. N. Owens, Co. A., 6th Regt. S. C. V. who fell mortally wounded at the battle of the Wilderness, May 6, 1864 (poem)

Issue of February 1, 1865

Died at his residence in York District, S. C., on the 18th of January, Joseph Douglass Sr., in the 62nd year of his age...a native of Sumter District, S. C., but when a boy eight years old, his parents moved to York District, where Joseph was raised in the lap of piety...member of Ebenezerchurch, and a ruling elder... in the organization called Allison's Creek...leaves wife, five daughters and three sons....
On Friday, January 27, Micah Jenkins, infant son of Col. and Mrs. A. Coward....

Issue of February 15, 1865

Married in Mecklenburg Co., N. C.,on the 9th instant, by Rev. J. C. Burge, Mr. Dawson N. Mitchell and Miss Mary J. Sloan.
Died in Yorkville, S. C., on the 27th of January, 1865, Micah Jenkins Coward, aged one month and twenty-seven days....
Death of James E. Quinn, on 7th instant....

Issue of March 16, 1865

Married on the 7th inst., by J. D. P. Currence, Esq., Mr. Samuel C. Johnston, and Mrs. Margaret Robeson, all of York District.

Issue of March 23, 1865

Married on the 14th instant, by Rev. S. L. Watson, Mr. O. N. Youngblood and Miss E. H. Currence, both of this District.

Issue of March 29, 1865

Married on the 7th February at the residence of the bride's father, by Rev. M. Oates, Capt. J. B. Lyle, 5th Regiment, S. C. V., and Miss M. C., daughter of Mijamin McCarthur, of Limestone Springs, S. C.
On the 22nd of February, by Rev. J. A. Davies, Mr. John C. Jackson, and Miss E. C. Thomasson, all of this District.

Issue of April 12, 1865

Died on the 9th of March, Mrs. Violet Amanda Barron, wife of J. Leroy Barron, aged thirty-five years, six months and three days...member of the Associate Reformed Presbyterian Church, at Tirzah, York District, S. C....

Issue of April 19, 1865

Married on the 6th instant, by Rev. S. L. Watson, Sergt. W. A. J. McCallum and Miss Cynthia A., daughter of Maj. A. A. McKenzie.

Issue of April 26, 1865

Married on Monday, the 17th inst., by S. G. Brown, Esq., Mr. A. L. Cox, of Tennessee to Miss M. Hartness, youngest daughter of Capt. J. W. A. Hartness of this district.
On Tuesday the 18th by J. G. Enloe, Esq., Mr. John Sherer, to Miss M. J. Thomas, all of this District.
ON Thursday, the 20th, by Rev. R. Y. Russell, Mr. Robert Hays to Miss Sarah Kell, all of this District.

(No issue from May 10 till August 17, 1865)

Issue of August 17, 1865

Married in Yorkville, on the 11th instant, by Rev. L. A. Johnson, Lieut. J. S. R. Thomson, of Spartanburg, and Miss Martha Jane, second daughter of W. I. Clawson, of this place.
In Yorkville on the 2d instant, by Rev. J. Monroe Anderson, Mr. William A. Elam, of Mecklenburg Co., Virginia, and Miss Sophia Jane, eldest daughter of Mr. Joseph Herndon of Yorkville, S. C.
Died in Yorkville on the 7th of July last, William A. Latta, Esq., in the 55th year of his age.
In Yorkville, on the 31st ultimo, Charles, only son of Mr. William L. and Mrs. Mary F. Grist, aged 2 years, 3 months and 4 days.

Issue of August 31, 1865

Married in York District, on the 24th inst., at the bride's residence by the Rev. J. A. Davies, Mr. J. D. Enloe, of Bradesburg, Kentucky, and Miss Naomi Gladden, of York District.

Issue of September 7, 1865

Died inYorkville, S. C., July 30th, aged seven months, Charles Calhoun, son of James Watkins and Fanny Mason Cook.
Died at the residence of his father, in this District, on the 23d ultimo, John Nelson Barnett, from a wound received at Petersburg, aged 22 years and 8 months.
Married on the 29th ultimo, by Rev.S. L. Watson, Capt. Wm. Jackson and Miss Susan E. Jackson, all of this District.
In Yorkville, on the 5th inst., by Rev. J. H. Massabeau, Mr. J. Patrick Palmer and Miss Alice A. Steedman, all of this place.

Issue of September 21, 1865

Married in this District on Thursday, 14th inst., by Rev. O. A. Darby, Rev. L. A. Johnson, of the South Carolina Conference, and Miss Margaret Smith, of this District.
Died near Ebenezer, in this District, at the residence of her brother, Wm. J. Faris, August 11th, Miss Margaret Faris, aged 67 years.
Near Ebenezer, in this District, at the residence of her brother William J. Faris, September 1st, Miss Nancy Faris, aged 51 years.

Issue of September 28, 1865

Married on the evening of the 19th instant, at the house of the bride's father, by Rev. R. Lathan, Mr. J. W. Pierce, and

Miss M. J. Miller.
    On the 21st inst., by Rev. Mr. Harris, Mr. Wm. A. Rhea and
Miss Sarah J. Ingram, all of this District.
    On the 26th inst., at the residence of the bride's father,
by Rev. R. Lathan, Mr. J. Parks Wilson and Miss Mary Ellen
McElwee, all of this District.

Issue of October 5, 1865

    Married in this District on Thursday, the 21st inst., by
J. D. P. Currence, Esq., Mr. John J. Johnson of Griffin, County,
Georgia, and Miss Easter Louisa Wallace, of York District.
    On the 26th ultimo, by Rev. M. Oates, Mr. E. W. Smith, and
Miss E. L. Niselands, all of this District.
    On the 28th ultimo, by Rev. J. B. Massabeau, Mr. D. E.
Stevenson, of Arkansas, and Mrs. Amanda E. Clark, of York
District.
    On the 29th of August, at the residence of the bride's father,
by Rev. M. Oates, Mr. J. A. Hope and Miss Lizzie Whitesides, all
of this District.
    In Yorkville, on the 3d instant, by Rev. R. Y. Russell, Dr.
James F. Noland of Union District, and Miss Ione Sadler, of this
place.
    Died on the 28th ult., James Tate, aged 4 years and 9 months,
only son of D. A. A. and M. L. Watson....

Issue of October 12, 1865

    Death of James H. Witherspoon at Lancaster Court House on
Monday of last week...a member of the late Confederate Congress.
    Married on the 5th inst., by Rev. S. L. Watson, Mr. Hugh
Tate of this District, and Miss Margaret Sloan of Mecklenburg
County, N. C.

Issue of October 19, 1865

    Married on Thursday, the 5th inst., by Rev. W. W. Carothers,
Mr. Wm. N. Guy, and Miss Amanda Porter, both of Chester District.
    Died in Yorkville, on Friday, 13th inst., Mr. Jerome B.
Kerr, aged about 43 years.

Issue of October 26, 1865

    Married at the bride's residence on the 19th inst., by J. P.
Hood, Esq., Mr. John Montgomery and Miss Mary Sandlin, all of
this district.
    Died in Yorkville on Wednesday, Oct. 18, at the age of 34
years, Mrs. Eugenia V. Chazal, a native of Savannah, Ga., and
wife of Dr. J. P. Chazal, of Charleston.

Issue of November 2, 1865

    Married in Yorkville on the 26th ult., by Rev. L. A. Johnson,
Rev. J. B. Massabeau, of the South Carolina Conference, and Miss
Jailie E. Alexander, of Yorkville.
    By Rev. R. Y. Russel, on the 26th ult., at the residence of
the bride's father, Lieut. J. D. McConnell to Miss Sarah A.
Jaggers, all of this District.
    On the 3rd of October, at the residence of the bride's bro-
ther, by Rev. James T. McElhaney, Mr. W. A. Carson, and Miss

Mary S. McElhaney, all of this District.
Also, on the evening of the same day, at the residence of
Mr. James Poag, by Rev. James T. McElhaney, Mr. J. W. Isom, and
Mrs. M. E. Burton, all of this District.
On the 19th of October, at the residence of Mr. J. Isom, by
Rev. James T. McElhaney, Mr. J. M. Rawls, and Miss Nancy Isom,
all of this District.
On the same day, at the residence of Miss S. Poag, by Rev.
J. T. McElhaney, Mr. N. Johnston of Alabama, and Miss M. E. Poag,
of York District.
In Chester, on the 17th inst., by Rev. Mr. Jacobs, at the
residence of the bride's father, Mr. H. Baum of Camden, S. C.,
and Miss Evereyman, of that place.
Died at his residence in this District, on Saturday, the
23d of September, Mr. Andrew Francis Love, in the 52nd year of
his age...a ruling elder in his church....

Issue of November 9, 1865

Died on the 25th of September, near Corinth, Miss., Mr. D.
H. Aughey, of Typhoid fever...married Miss Catharine H. McElwee,
youngest daughter of Mr. James McElwee, of this District....

Issue of November 16, 1865

Married on Thursday evening, 9th inst., by Rev. W. W. Caro-
thers, Mr. Leander Pardue of Chester District, and Miss Sarah
Ann, daughter of D. McElmoyle, of this District.
In Chester, on the 31st inst., Mr. S. M. McDill and Miss
M. E. McDaniel,all of that district.

Issue of November 23, 1865

Married by Rev. S. L. Watson, on the 14th inst., Mr. Robert
Harper and Miss Margaret Dameron, all of this District.
Also, by the same on the same day, Maj. S. N. Stowe and
Miss Sophia M. Ford, both of Gaston County, N. C.
On the 14th inst., by Rev. W. W. Carothers, Mr. Wm. F.
Garrison, and Miss Nancy H., daughter of David Poovey, all of
this district.
At the house of the bride's father, on the evening of the 16th
inst., by the Rev. B. Latham, Mr. J. Templeton Hall and Miss
M. E. Killian, all of this District.
Died at her residence near Monticello, Fairfield District,
at three o'clock, on Tuesday morning, the 14th inst., Mrs. Mary
C., wife of John Willingham, and daughter of Wylie L. and C. H.
Harris, of York District.
At Yorkville, on the 1st inst., Margaret Eugenia, fourth
daughter of Charles P. and M. Octavia Almar, aged four years,
one month and eighteen days.

Issue of November 30, 1865

Married on the 23rd instant, by Rev. S. L. Watson, Capt.
G. A. Patrick and Mrs. M. M. Riddle, all of this District.
On the 3d of October by Rev. J. T. McElhaney, Mr. W. J. Isom
and Miss Martha J. Poag, all of this district.

Issue of December 7, 1865

Died on the 28th ult., Laura Catharine, youngest daughter of
L. B. and J. A. J. Sherrer, aged 1 year, 7 months and 3 days.

Issue of December 14, 1865

Married on Tuesday evening, 5th inst., by Rev. W. W. Carothers, Mr. William M. Finley and Miss Jane E., daughter of Peter
McCallum, all of this district.

At the house of Mrs. F. L. Workman, on the 7th inst., Mr.
Wm. A. Steele and Miss Sarah E. Boyd, all of York District.

At the residence of the bride's mother, on Tuesday, 5th
inst., by Rev. R. Y. Russel, Mr. G. L. McNeel and Miss Mary
Davidson, all of this District.

On the 30th ult., by Rev. S. L. Watson, Mr. M. L. Sifford
and Miss R. Erxina McKenzie, all of this district.

Issue of December 21, 1865

Died at Point Lookout, Sergt. H. G. Caldwell, of Co. K.,
17th S. C. Vol. aged 23 years....

Died in Charleston, on the 8th inst., Mary Claudia, third
daughter of Charles P. and M. Octavia Almar, aged seven years,
two months and one day.

INDEX

CPSIA information can be obtained
at www.ICGtesting.com
Printed in the USA
BVHW032108250721
612393BV00005B/58